INDIAN HOME RULE

BY
M. K. GANDHI

Being a Translation of "HIND SWARAJ"
(Indian Home Rule), published in the Gujarati
columns of INDIAN OPINION,
11th and 18th Dec.,
1909

No Rights Reserved

INTERNATIONAL PRINTING PRESS
PHOENIX, NATAL
1910

* This book has been published as is with limited to no editorial intervention.

CONTENTS

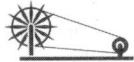

PREFACE TO THE ENGLISH TRANSLATION

It is not without hesitation that the translation of "HIND SWARAJ" is submitted to the public.[1] A European friend,[2] with whom I discussed the contents, wanted to see a translation of it and, during our spare moments, I hurriedly dictated and he took it down. It is not a literal translation but it is a faithful rendering of the original.[3] Several English friends have read it, and whilst opinions were being invited as to the advisability of publishing the work, news was received that the original was seized in India. This information hastened the decision to publish the translation without a moment's delay. My fellow-workers at the International Printing Press[4] shared my view and, by working overtime—a labour of love—they have enabled me to place the translation before the public in an unexpectedly short time. The work is being given to the public at what is practically cost-price. But, without the financial assistance of the many Indians who promised to buy copies for themselves and for distribution, it might never have seen the light of day.

I am quite aware of the many imperfections in the original. The English rendering, besides sharing these, must naturally exaggerate them, owing to my inability to convey the exact meaning of the original. Some of the friends who have read the translation have objected that the subject matter has been dealt with in the form of a dialogue. I have no answer to offer to this objection except that the Gujarati language readily lends itself to such treatment and that it is considered the best method of treating difficult subjects. Had I written for English readers in the first instance, the subject would have been handled in a different manner. Moreover, the dialogue, as it has been given, actually took place between several friends, mostly readers of INDIAN OPINION,[5] and myself.

Whilst the views expressed in "HIND SWARAJ" are held by me, I have but endeavoured humbly to follow Tolstoy,[6] Ruskin,[7] Thoreau,[8] Emerson[9] and other writers, besides the masters of Indian philosophy. Tolstoy has been one of my teachers for a number of years. Those who want to see a corroboration of the views submitted in the following chapters, will find it in the works of the above-named masters. For ready reference, some of the books are mentioned in the Appendices.

I do not know why "HIND SWARAJ" has been seized in India. To me, the seizure constitutes further condemnation of the civilisation represented by the British Government.[10] There is in the book not a trace of approval of violence in any shape or form. The methods of the British Government are, undoubtedly, severely condemned. To do otherwise would be for me to be a traitor to Truth, to India, and to the Empire to which I own allegiance. My notion of loyalty does not involve acceptance of current rule or government irrespective of its righteousness or otherwise. Such notion is based upon the belief—not in its present justice or morality but—in a future acceptance by governments of that standard of morality in practice which it at present vaguely and hypocritically believes in, in theory. But I must frankly confess that I am not so much concerned about the stability of the Empire as I am about that of the ancient civilisation of India which, in my opinion, represents the best that the world has ever seen. The British Government in India constitutes a struggle between the Modern Civilisation, which is the Kingdom of Satan, and the Ancient Civilisation, which is the Kingdom of God. The one is the God of War, the other is the God of Love. My countrymen impute the evils of modern civilisation to the English people and, therefore, believe that the English people are bad, and not the civilisation they represent. My countrymen, therefore, believe that they should adopt modern civilisation and modern methods of violence to drive out the English. "HIND SWARAJ" has been written in order to show that they are following a suicidal policy, and that, if they would but revert to their own glorious civilisation, either the English would adopt the latter and become Indianised or find their occupation in India gone.

It was at first intended to publish the translation as a part of INDIAN OPINION, but the seizure of the original rendered such a course inadvisable. INDIAN OPINION represents the Transvaal Passive Resistance struggle and ventilates the grievances of British Indians in South Africa generally. It was, therefore, thought desirable not to publish through a representative organ, views which are held by me personally and which may even be considered dangerous or disloyal. I am naturally anxious not to compromise a great struggle by any action of mine which has no connection with it. Had I not known that there was a danger of methods of violence becoming popular, even in South Africa, had I not been called upon by hundreds of my countrymen, and not a few English friends, to express my opinion on the Nationalist movement in India, I would even have refrained, for the sake of the struggle, from reducing my views to writing. But, occupying the position I do, it would have been cowardice on my part to postpone publication under the circumstances just referred to.

M.K. GANDHI
Johannesburg,
March 20th, 1910

FOREWORD

I have written some chapters[1] on the subject of Indian Home Rule which I venture to place[2] before the readers of INDIAN OPINION. I have written because I could not restrain myself. I have read much, I have pondered much, during the stay, for four months in London of the Transvaal Indian deputation. I discussed things with as many of my countrymen as I could. I met, too, as many Englishmen as it was possible for me to meet. I consider it my duty now to place before the readers of INDIAN OPINION the conclusions, which appear to me to be final. The Gujarati subscribers of INDIAN OPINION number about 800. I am aware that, for every subscriber, there are at least ten persons who read the paper with zest. Those who cannot read Gujarati have the paper read to them. Such persons have often questioned me about the condition of India. Similar questions were addressed to me in London. I felt, therefore, that it might not be improper for me to ventilate publicly the views expressed by me in private.

These views are mine, and yet not mine. They are mine because I hope to act according to them. They are almost a part of my being. But, yet, they are not mine, because I lay no claim to originality. They have been formed after reading several books. That which I dimly felt received support from these books.

The views I venture to place before the reader, are needless to say, held by many Indians not touched by what is known as civilisation, but I ask the reader to believe me when I tell him that they are also held by thousands of Europeans. Those who wish to dive deep, and have time, may read certain books themselves. If time permits me, I hope to translate portions of such books for the benefit of the readers of INDIAN OPINION.

If the readers of INDIAN OPINION and others who may see the following chapters will pass their criticism on to me, I shall feel obliged to them.

The only motive is to serve my country, to find out the Truth, and to follow it. If, therefore, my views are proved to be wrong, I shall have no hesitation in rejecting them. If they are proved to be right, I would naturally wish, for the sake of the Motherland, that others should adopt them.

To make it easy reading, the chapters are written in the form of a dialogue[3] between the reader[4] and the editor.[5]

M. K. GANDHI[6]
Kildonan Castle,
November 22nd, 1909.

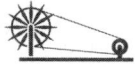

1

INDIAN HOME RULE[1]

The Congress and its Officials[2]

READER: Just at present there is a Home Rule wave[3] passing over India. All our countrymen appear to be pining for National Independence. A similar spirit pervades them even in South Africa. Indians seem to be eager after acquiring rights.[4] Will you explain your views in this matter?

EDITOR: You have well put the question, but the answer is not easy.[5] One of the objects of a newspaper is to understand the popular feeling and to give expression to it; another is to arouse among the people certain desirable sentiments; and the third is fearlessly to expose popular defects.[6] The exercise of all these three functions is involved in answering your question. To a certain extent, the people's will has to be expressed; certain sentiments will need to be fostered, and defects will have to be brought to light. But, as you have asked the question, it is my duty to answer it.

READER: Do you then consider that a desire for Home Rule has been created among us?

EDITOR: That desire gave rise to the National Congress. The choice of the word "National" implies it.

READER: That, surely, is not the case. Young India seems to ignore the Congress. It is considered to be an instrument for perpetuating British Rule.

EDITOR: That opinion is not justified. Had not the Grand Old Man of India prepared the soil, our young men could not have even spoken about Home Rule. How can we forget what Mr. Hume has written, how he has lashed us into action, and with what effort he has awakened us, in order to achieve the objects of the Congress? Sir William Wedderburn has given his body, mind and money to the same cause. His writings are worthy of perusal to this day. Professor Gokhale, in order to prepare the Nation, embraced poverty and gave twenty years of his life.[7] Even now, he is living in poverty. The late Justice Buddrudin Tyebji[8] was also one of those who, through the Congress, sowed the seed of Home Rule. Similarly, in Bengal, Madras, the Punjab and other places, there have been lovers of India and members of the Congress, both Indian and English.

READER: Stay, stay, you are going too far, you are straying away from my question. I have asked you about Home or Self-Rule; you are discussing foreign rule. I do not desire to hear English names, and you are giving me such names. In these circumstances, I do not think we can ever meet. I shall be pleased if you will confine yourself to Home Rule. All other wise talk will not satisfy me.

EDITOR: You are impatient. I cannot afford to be likewise. If you will bear with me for a while, I think you will find that you will obtain what you want. Remember the old proverb that the tree does not grow in one day.[9] The fact that you have checked me, and that you do not want to hear about the well-wishers of India, shows that, for you at any rate, Home Rule is yet far away.[10] If we had many like you, we would never make any advance. This thought is worthy of your attention.

READER: It seems to me that you simply want to put me off by talking round and round. Those whom you consider to be well-wishers of India are not such in my estimation. Why, then, should I listen to your discourse on such people? What has he whom you consider to be the father of the nation[11] done for it? He says that the English Governors will do justice, and that we should co-operate with them.

EDITOR: I must tell you, with all gentleness, that it must be a matter of shame for us that you should speak about that great man in terms of disrespect. Just look at his work. He has dedicated his life to the service of India. We have learned what we know from him. It was the respected Dadabhai[12] who taught us that the English had sucked our life-blood. What does it matter that, to-day, his trust is still in the English nation? Is Dadabhai less to be honoured because, in the exuberance of youth, we are prepared to go a step further? Are we, on that account, wiser than he? It is a mark of wisdom not to kick against the very step from which we have risen higher.[13] The removal of a step from a staircase brings down the whole of it. When, out of infancy, we grow into youth, we do not despise infancy, but, on the contrary, we recall with affection the days of our childhood. If, after many years of study, a teacher were to teach me something, and if I were to build a little more on the foundation laid by that teacher, I would not, on that account, be considered wiser than the teacher. He would always command my respect. Such is the case with the Grand Old Man of India.[14] We must admit that he is the author of Nationalism.[15]

READER: You have spoken well. I can now understand that we must look upon Mr. Dadabhai with respect. Without him and men like him, we would[16] probably not have the spirit that fires us. How can the same be said of Professor Gokhale?[17] He has constituted himself a great friend of the English; he says that we have to learn a great deal from them, that we have to learn their political wisdom, before we can talk of Home Rule.[18] I am tired of reading his speeches.

EDITOR: If you are tired, it only betrays your impatience. We believe that those who are discontented with the slowness of their parents, and are angry because the parents would not run with their children, are considered disrespectful to their parents.[19] Professor Gokhale occupies the place of a parent. What does it matter if he cannot run with us? A nation that is desirous of securing Home Rule cannot afford to despise its ancestors. We shall become useless, if we lack respect for our elders. Only men with mature thoughts are capable of ruling themselves, and not the hasty-tempered. Moreover, how many Indians were there like Professor Gokhale, when he gave himself to Indian education? I verily believe that whatever Professor Gokhale does he does with pure motives and with a view to serving India. His devotion to the Motherland is so great, that he would give his life for it, if necessary.[20] Whatever he says is said not to flatter anyone but because he believes it to be true. We are bound, therefore, to entertain the highest regard for him.

READER: Are we, then, to follow him in every respect?

EDITOR: I never said any such thing. If we conscientiously differed from him, the learned Professor himself would advise us to follow the dictates of our conscience rather than him. Our chief purpose is not to cry down his work, but to believe that he is infinitely greater than we, and to feel assured that compared with his work for India, ours is infinitesimal.[21] Several newspapers write disrespectfully of him. It is our duty to protest against such writings. We should consider men like Professor Gokhale to be the pillars of Home Rule. It is a bad habit to say that another man's thoughts are bad and ours only are good, and that those holding different views from ours are the enemies of the country.[22]

READER: I now begin to understand somewhat your meaning. I shall have to think the matter over, but what you say about Mr. Hume and Sir William Wedderburn[23] is beyond comprehension.[24]

EDITOR: The same rule holds good for the English as for the Indians. I can never subscribe to the statement that all Englishmen are bad. Many Englishmen desire Home Rule[25] for India. That the English people are somewhat more selfish than others is true, but that does not prove that every Englishman is bad. We who seek justice will have to do justice to others. Sir William does not wish ill to India—that should be enough for us. As we proceed, you will see that if we act justly, India will be sooner free. You will see, too, that, if we shun every Englishman as an enemy, Home Rule will be delayed. But if we are just to them, we shall receive their support in our progress towards the goal.

READER: All this seems to me at present to be simply nonsensical. English support and the obtaining of Home Rule[26] are two contradictory things. How can the English people tolerate Home Rule for us? But I do not want you to decide this question for me just yet. To pass time over it is useless.[27] When you have shown how we can have Home Rule,[28] perhaps I shall understand your views. You have prejudiced me against you by discoursing on English help. I would, therefore, beseech you not to continue this subject.

EDITOR: I have no desire to do so. That you are prejudiced against me is not a matter for much anxiety. It is well that I should say unpleasant things at the commencement, it is my duty patiently to try to remove your prejudice.[29]

READER: I like that last statement. It emboldens me to say what I like. One thing still puzzles me. I do not understand how the Congress laid the foundation of Home Rule.[30]

EDITOR: Let us see. The Congress brought together Indians from different parts of India and enthused us with the idea of Nationality. The Government used to look upon it with disfavour. The Congress has always insisted that the Nation[31] should control revenue and expenditure. It has always desired self-government after the Canadian model. Whether we can get it or not, whether we desire it or not, and whether there is not something more desirable, are different questions. All I have to show is that the Congress gave us a fore-taste[32] of Home Rule. To deprive it of the honour is not proper, and for us to do so would not only be ungrateful but retard the fulfilment of our object. To treat the Congress as an institution inimical to our growth as a Nation[33] would disable us from using that body.[34]

2

THE PARTITION OF BENGAL[1]

READER: Considering the matter as you put it, it seems proper to say that the foundation of Home Rule was laid by the Congress. But you will admit that it cannot be considered a real awakening. When and how did the real awakening[2] take place?

EDITOR: The seed is never seen. It works underneath the ground, is itself destroyed, and the tree which rises above the ground is alone seen. Such is the case with the Congress. Yet, what you call the real awakening took place after the Partition of Bengal. For this, we have to be thankful to Lord Curzon. At the time of the Partition, the people of Bengal reasoned with Lord Curzon, but, in the pride of power, he disregarded all their prayers, he took it for granted that Indians could only prattle, that they could never take any effective steps.[3] He used insulting language, and, in the teeth of all opposition, partitioned Bengal.[4] That day may be considered to be the day of the partition of the British Empire. The shock that the British power received through the Partition has never been equalled by any other act. This does not mean that the other injustices done to India are less glaring than that done by the Partition. The salt-tax is not a small injustice. We shall see many such things later on. But the people were ready to resist the Partition. At that time, the feeling ran high.[5] Many leading Bengalis were ready to lose their all. They knew their power; hence the conflagration. It is now well nigh unquenchable; it is not necessary to quench it either. Partition will go, Bengal will be re-united, but the rift in the English barque will remain; it must daily widen.[6] India awakened is not likely to fall asleep. Demand for abrogation of Partition is tantamount to demand for Home Rule.[7] Leaders in Bengal know this, British officials realise it. That is why Partition still remains. As time passes, the Nation is being forged. Nations are not formed in a day; the formation requires years.

READER: What, in your opinion, are the results of Partition?

EDITOR: Hitherto we have considered that, for redress of grievances, we must approach the Throne, and, if we get no redress, we must sit still, except that we may still petition.[8] After the Partition, people saw that petitions must be backed up by force.[9] and that they must be capable of suffering. This new spirit[10] must be considered to be the chief result of Partition. That spirit was seen in the outspoken writings in the press.[11] That which the people said tremblingly and in secret began to be said and to be written publicly. The Swadeshi movement was inaugurated. People, young and old, used to run away at the sight of an English face; it now no longer awed them.[12] They did not fear even a row, or being imprisoned. Some of the best sons of India[13] are at present in banishment. This is something different from mere petitioning. Thus are the people moved. The spirit generated in

Bengal has spread in the North to the Punjab, and, in the South, to Cape Comorin.[14]

READER: Do you suggest any other striking result?

EDITOR: The Partition has not only made a rift in the English ship, but has made it in ours also. Great events always produce great results. Our leaders are divided into two parties: the moderates and the extremists. These may be considered as the slow party and the impatient party. Some call the moderates the timid party, and the extremists the bold party.[15] All interpret the two words according to their preconceptions. This much is certain that there has arisen an enmity between the two. The one distrusts the other, and imputes motives. At the time of the Surat Congress, there was almost a fight. I think that this division is not a good thing for the country, but I think also that such divisions will not last long.[16] It all depends upon the leaders how long they will last.

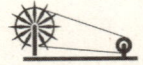

3

DISCONTENT AND UNREST

READER: Then you consider Partition[1] to be a cause of the awakening? Do you welcome the unrest which has resulted from it?

EDITOR: When a man rises from sleep, he twists his limbs and is restless. It takes some time before he is entirely awakened. Similarly, although the Partition has caused an awakening, the comatose state has not yet disappeared. We are still twisting our limbs and still restless, and just as the state between sleep and awakening must be considered to be necessary, so may the present unrest in India be considered a necessary and, therefore, a proper state. The knowledge that there is unrest will, it is highly probable, enable us to outgrow it. Rising from sleep. we do not continue in a comatose state, but, according to our ability, sooner or later, we are completely restored to our senses. So shall we be free from the present unrest which no one likes.[2]

READER: What is the other form of unrest?

EDITOR: Unrest is, in reality, discontent. The latter is only now described as unrest. During the Congress-period, it was labelled discontent; Mr. Hume always said that the spread of discontent in India was necessary. This discontent is a very useful thing. So long as a man is contented with his present lot, so long is it difficult to persuade him to come out of it.[3] Therefore it is that every reform must be preceded by discontent. We throw away things we have, only when we cease to like them. Such discontent has been produced among us after reading the great works of Indians and Englishmen. Discontent has led to unrest, and the latter has brought about many deaths, many imprisonments, many banishments. Such a state of things will still continue. It must be so. All these may be considered good signs, but they may also lead to bad results.

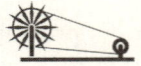

4

WHAT IS SWARAJ?

READER: I have now learnt what the Congress has done to make India one nation, how the Partition has caused an awakening, and how discontent and unrest have spread through the land. I would now like to know your views on Swaraj. I fear that our interpretation is not the same.[1]

EDITOR: It is quite possible that we do not attach the same meaning to the term. You and I and all Indians are impatient to obtain Swaraj, but we are certainly not decided as to what it is. To drive the English out of India is a thought heard from many mouths, but it does not seem that many have properly considered why it should be so. I must ask you a question. Do you think that it is necessary to drive away the English, if we get all we want?

READER: I should ask of them only one thing, that is: "Please leave our country." If after they have complied with this request, their withdrawal from India means that they are still in India, I should have no objection. Then we would understand that, in our language, the word "gone" is equivalent to "remained".[2]

12

EDITOR: Well, then, let us suppose that the English have retired.[3] What will you do then?

READER: That question cannot be answered at this stage. The state after withdrawal will depend largely upon the manner of it. If, as you assume, they retire, it seems to me we shall still keep their constitution, and shall carry on the government. If they simply retire for the asking, we should have an army, etc., ready at hand. We should, therefore, have no difficulty in carrying on the government.[4]

EDITOR: You may think so: I do not. But I will not discuss the matter just now. I have to answer your question, and that I can do well by asking you several questions. Why do we want to drive away the English?[5]

READER: Because India has become impoverished by their Government. They take away our money from year to year. The most important posts are reserved for themselves. We are kept in a state of slavery. They behave insolently towards us, and disregard our feelings.

EDITOR: If they do not take our money away, become gentle, and give us responsible posts, would you still consider their presence to be harmful?

READER: That question is useless. It is similar to the question whether there is any harm in associating with a tiger, if he changes his nature. Such a question is sheer waste of time. When a tiger changes his nature, Englishmen will change theirs. This is not possible, and to believe it to be possible is contrary to human experience.

EDITOR: Supposing we get self-government similar to what the Canadians and the South Africans have, will it be good enough?[6]

READER: That question also is useless. We may get it when we have arms and ammunition even as they have. But, when we have the same powers, we shall hoist our own flag. As is Japan, so must India be. We must own our navy, our army, and we must have our own splendour, and then will India's voice ring through the world.[7]

EDITOR: You have well drawn the picture.[8] In effect, it means this: that we want English rule without the Englishman. You want the tiger's nature, but not the tiger; that is to say, you would make India English, and, when it becomes English, it will be called not Hindustan but Englistan.[9] This is not the Swaraj that I want.

READER: I have placed before you my idea of Swaraj as I think it should be. If the education we have received be of any use, if the works of Spencer, Mill and others be of any importance, and if the English Parliament be the Mother of Parliaments, I certainly think that we should copy the English people, and this to such an extent, that, just as they do not allow others to obtain a footing in their country, so should we not allow them or others to obtain it in ours.[10] What they have done in their own country has not been done in any other country. It is, therefore, proper for us to import their institutions. But now I want to know your views.

EDITOR: There is need for patience.[11] My views will develop of themselves in the course of this discourse. It is as difficult for me to understand the true nature of Swaraj as it seems to you to be easy. I shall, therefore, for the time being, content myself with endeavouring to show that what you call Swaraj is not truly Swaraj.[12]

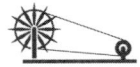

5

THE CONDITION OF ENGLAND

READER: Then from your statement I deduce that the Government of England is not desirable and not worth copying by us.

EDITOR: Your deduction is justified. The condition of England at present is pitiable. I pray to God that India may never be in that plight. That which you consider to be the Mother of Parliaments is like a sterile woman and a prostitute.[1] Both these are harsh terms, but exactly fit the case. That Parliament has not yet of its own accord done a single good thing, hence I have compared it to a sterile woman.[2] The natural condition of that Parliament is such that, without outside pressure, it can do nothing. It is like a prostitute because it is under the control of ministers who change from time to time. Today it is under Mr. Asquith, tomorrow it may be under Mr. Balfour.

READER: You have said this sarcastically. The term "sterile woman" is not applicable. The Parliament, being elected by the people, must work under public pressure. This is its quality.

EDITOR: You are mistaken. Let us examine it a little more closely. The best men are supposed to be elected by the people. The members serve without pay and, therefore, it must be assumed, only for the public weal. The electors are considered to be educated and, therefore, we should assume that they would not generally make mistakes in their choice.[3] Such a Parliament should not need the spur of petitions or any other pressure. Its work should be so smooth that its effect[4] would be more apparent day by day. But, as a matter of fact, it is generally acknowledged that the members are hypocritical and selfish. Each thinks of his own little interest. It is fear that is the guiding motive. What is done to-day may be undone to-morrow. It is not possible to recall a single instance in which finality can be predicated for its work. When the greatest questions are debated, its members have been seen to stretch themselves and to dose. Sometimes the members talk away until the listeners are disgusted. Carlyle has called it the "talking-shop of the world".[5] Members vote for their party without a thought. Their so-called discipline binds them to it. If any member, by way of exception, gives an independent vote, he is considered a renegade. If the money and the time wasted by the Parliament were entrusted to a few good men, the English nation would be occupying to-day a much higher platform.[6] The Parliament is simply a costly toy of the nation. These views are by no means peculiar to me. Some great English thinkers have expressed them. One of the members of that Parliament recently said that a true Christian[7] could not become a member of it. Another said that it was a baby. And, if it has remained a baby after an existence of seven hundred years, when will it outgrow its babyhood?

READER: You have set me thinking; you do not expect me to accept at once all you say. You give me entirely novel views.

I shall have to digest them. Will you now explain the epithet "prostitute"?[8]

EDITOR: That you cannot accept my views at once is only right. If you will read the literature on this subject, you will have some idea of it. The Parliament is without a real master. Under the Prime Minister, its movement is not steady, but it is buffeted about like a prostitute. The Prime Minister is more concerned about his power than about the welfare of the Parliament. His energy is concentrated upon securing the success of his party. His care is not always that the Parliament shall do right, Prime Ministers are known to have made the Parliament do things merely for party advantage. All this is worth thinking over.[9]

READER: Then you are really attacking the very men whom we have hitherto considered to be patriotic and honest?

EDITOR: Yes, that is true; I can have nothing against Prime Ministers, but what I have seen leads me to think that they cannot be considered really patriotic. If they are to be considered honest because they do not take what is generally known as bribery, let them be so considered, but they are open to subtler influences.[10] In order to gain their ends, they certainly bribe people with honours. I do not hesitate to say that they have neither real honesty nor a living conscience.

READER: As you express these views about the Parliament,[11] I would like to hear you on the English people, so that I may have your view of their Government.[12]

EDITOR: To the English voters, their newspaper is their Bible.[13] They take their cue from their newspapers, which latter are often dishonest.[14] The same fact is differently interpreted by different newspapers, according to the party in whose interests they are edited. One newspaper would consider a great Englishman to be a paragon of honesty, another would consider him dishonest. What must be the condition of the people whose newspapers are of this type?

READER: You shall describe it.

EDITOR: These people change their views frequently. It is said that they change them every even years. These views swing like the pendulum of a clock and are never steadfast. The people would follow a powerful orator or a man who gives them parties, receptions, etc. As are the people, so is their Parliament. They have certainly one quality very strongly developed. They will never allow their country to be lost. If any person were to cast an evil eye on it, they would pluck out his eyes. But that does not mean that the nation possesses every other virtue or that it should be imitated. If India copies England, it is my firm conviction that she will be ruined.

READER: To what do you ascribe this state of England?

EDITOR: It is not due to any peculiar fault of the English people, but the condition is due to modern civilisation. It is a civilisation only in name.[15] Under it, the nations of Europe are becoming degraded and ruined day by day.

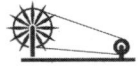

6

CIVILISATION[1]

READER: Now you will have to explain what you mean by civilisation.[2]

EDITOR: It is not a question of what I mean. Several English writers refuse to call that civilisation which passes under that name. Many books have been written upon that subject. Societies have been formed to cure the nation of the evils of civilisation. A great English writer has written a work called "Civilisation: its Cause and Cure".[3] Therein he has called it a disease.

READER: Why do we not know this generally?

EDITOR: The answer is very simple. We rarely find people arguing against themselves. Those who are intoxicated by modern civilisation are not likely to write against it. Their care will be to find out facts and arguments in support of it, and this they do unconsciously, believing it to be true. A man, whilst he is dreaming, believes in his dream he is undeceived only when he is awakened from his sleep. A man labouring under the bane of civilisation is like a dreaming man. What we usually read are the works of defenders of modern civilisation, which undoubtedly claim among its votaries very brilliant and even some very good men. Their writings hypnotise us. And so, one by one, we are drawn into the vortex.

READER: This seems to be very plausible. Now will you tell me something of what you have read and thought of this civilisation?

EDITOR: Let us first consider what state of things is described by the word "civilisation". Its true test lies in the fact that people living in it make bodily welfare the object of life.[4] We will take some examples. The people of Europe to-day live in better-built houses than they did a hundred years ago. This is considered an emblem of civilisation, and this is also a matter to promote bodily happiness. Formerly, they wore skins, and used as their weapons spears.[5] Now, they wear long trousers, and, for embellishing their bodies, they wear a variety of clothing, and, instead of spears, they carry with them revolvers containing five or more chambers. If people of a certain country, who have hitherto not been in the habit of wearing much clothing, boots, etc., adopt European clothing, they are supposed to have become civilised out of savagery. Formerly, in Europe, people ploughed their lands mainly by manual labour. Now, one man can plough a vast tract by means of steam-engines,[6] and can thus amass great wealth. This is called a sign of civilisation. Formerly, the fewest men wrote books that were most valuable.[7] Now, anybody writes and prints anything he likes and poisons people's minds. Formerly, men travelled in waggons: they fly now through the air in trains at the rate of four hundred and more miles per day. This is considered the height of civilisation. It has been stated that, as men progress, they shall be able to travel in airships and reach any part of the world in a few hours. Men will not need the use of their hands and feet. They will press a button, and they will have their clothing by their side. They will press another button, and they will have their newspaper. A third, and a motor-car will be in waiting for them. They will have a variety of delicately dished-up food.[8] Everything will be done by machinery. Formerly, when people wanted to fight with one another, they measured between them their bodily strength; now it is possible to take away thousands of lives by one man working behind a gun from a hill. This is civilisation. Formerly, men worked in the open air only so much as they liked.[9] Now, thousands[10] of workmen meet together and for the sake of maintenance work in factories or mines. Their condition is worse than that of beasts. They are obliged to work, at the risk of their lives, at most dangerous occupations,[11] for the sake of millionaires. Formerly, men were made slaves under physical compulsion, now they are enslaved by temptation of money and of the luxuries that money can buy.[12] There are now diseases of which people never dreamt before, and an army of doctors is engaged in finding out their cures, and so hospitals have increased. This is a test of civilisation. Formerly, special messengers were required and much expense was incurred in order to send letters; to-day, anyone can abuse his fellow by means of a letter for one penny. True, at the same cost, one can send one's thanks also. Formerly, people had two or three meals consisting of home-made bread and vegetables; now, they require something to eat every two hours, so that they have hardly leisure for anything else.[13] What more need I say? All this you can ascertain from several authoritative books. These are all true tests of civilisation. And, if anyone speaks to the contrary, know that he is ignorant. This civilisation takes note neither of morality nor of religion. Its votaries calmly state that their business is not to teach religion. Some even consider it to be a superstitious growth. Others put on the cloak of religion, and prate about morality.

But, after twenty years' experience, I have come to the conclusion that immorality is often taught in the name of morality. Even a child can understand that in all I have described above there can be no inducement to morality. Civilisation seeks to increase bodily comforts, and it fails miserably even in doing so.

This civilisation is irreligion, and it has taken such a hold on the people in Europe that those who are in it appear to be half-mad.[14] They lack real physical strength or courage. They keep up their energy by intoxication. They can hardly be happy in solitude. Women, who should be the queens of households, wander in the streets, or they[15] slave away in factories. For the sake of a pittance, half a million women in England alone are labouring under trying circumstances in factories or similar institutions. This awful fact is one of the causes of the daily growing suffragette movement. This civilisation is such that one has only to be patient and it will be self-destroyed. According to the teaching of Mahomed, this would be considered a Satanic civilisation. Hinduism calls it the Black Age. I cannot give you an adequate conception of it. It is eating into the vitals of the English nation. It must be shunned. Parliaments are really emblems of slavery. If you will sufficiently think over this, you will entertain the same opinion, and cease to blame the English. They rather deserve our sympathy. They are a shrewd nation and I, therefore, believe that they will cast off the evil. They are enterprising and industrious, and their mode of thought is not inherently immoral. Neither are they bad at heart. I, therefore, respect them. Civilisation is not an incurable disease, but it should never be forgotten that the English people are at present afflicted by it.[16]

7

WHY WAS INDIA LOST?

READER: You have said much about civilisation—enough to make me ponder over it. I do not now know what I should adopt and what I should avoid from the nations of Europe, but one question comes to my lips immediately. If civilisation is a disease, and if it has attacked the English nation, why has she been able to take India, and why is she able to retain it?[1]

EDITOR: Your question is not very difficult to answer, and we shall presently be able to examine the true nature of Swaraj; for I am aware that I have still to answer that question.[2] I will, however, take up your previous question. The English have not taken India; we[3] have given it to them. They are not in India because of their strength, but because we keep them. Let us now see whether these pro-positions can be sustained. They came to our country originally for purposes of trade. Recall the Company Bahadur. Who made it Bahadur? They had not the slightest intention at the time of establishing a kingdom. Who assisted the Company's officers? Who was tempted at the sight of their silver?

Who bought their goods? History testifies that we did all this. In order to become rich all at once, we welcomed the Company's officers with open arms. We assisted them. If I am in the habit of drinking bhang,[4] and a seller thereof sells it to me, am I to blame him or myself? By blaming the seller shall I be able to avoid the habit? And, if a particular retailer is driven away, will not another take his place? A true servant of India will have to go to the root of the matter. If an excess of food has caused me indigestion, I will certainly not avoid it by blaming water. He is a true physician who probes the cause of disease, and, if you[5] pose as a physician for the disease of India, you will have to find out its true cause.

READER: You are right. Now, I think[6] you will not have to argue much with me to drive your conclusions home. I am impatient to know your further views. We are now on a most interesting topic. I shall, therefore, endeavour to follow your thought, and stop you when I am in doubt.

EDITOR: I am afraid that, in spite of your enthusiasm, as we proceed further[7] we shall have differences of opinion. Nevertheless, I shall argue only when you will stop me.[8] We have already seen that the English merchants were able to get a footing in India because we encouraged them. When our princes[9] fought among themselves, they sought the assistance of Company Bahadur. That corporation was versed alike in commerce and war. It was unhampered by questions of morality. Its object was to increase its commerce and to make money. It accepted our assistance, and increased the number of its warehouses. To protect the latter, it employed an army which was utilised by us also. Is it not then useless to blame the English for what we did at that time? The Hindus and the Mahomedans were at daggers drawn. This, too, gave the Company its opportunity, and thus we created the circumstances that gave the Company its control over India. Hence it is truer to say that we gave India to the English than that India was lost.

READER: Will you now tell me how they are able to retain India?

EDITOR: The causes that gave them India enable them to retain it. Some Englishmen state that they took, and they hold, India by the sword.[10] Both these statements are wrong. The sword is entirely useless for holding India. We alone keep them. Napoleon is said to have described the English as a nation of shop keepers.[11] It is a fitting description. They hold whatever dominions sake of their commerce. Their army and their navy are intended to protect it. When the Transvaal offered no such attractions, the late Mr. Gladstone discovered that it was not right for the English to hold it. When it became a paying proposition, resistance led to war. Mr. Chamberlain soon discovered that England enjoyed a suzerainty over the Transvaal. It is related that someone asked the late President Kruger whether there was gold in the moon?[12] He replied that it was highly unlikely, because, if there were, the English would have annexed it. Many problems can be solved by remembering that money is their God. Then it follows that we keep the English in India for our base self-interest. We like their commerce, they please us by their subtle methods, and[13] get what they want from us. To blame them for this is to perpetuate their power. We further strengthen their hold by quarrelling amongst ourselves. If you accept the above statements, it is proved that the English entered India for the purposes of trade. They remain in it for the same purpose, and[14] we help them to do so. Their arms and ammunition are perfectly useless. In this connection, I remind you that it is the British flag which is waving in Japan, and not the Japanese.[15] The English have a treaty with Japan for the sake of their commerce, and you will see that, if they can manage it, their commerce will greatly expand in that country.[16] They wish to convert the whole world into a vast market for their goods. That they cannot do so is true, but the blame will not be theirs. They will leave no stone unturned to reach the goal.

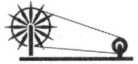

8

THE CONDITION OF INDIA[1]

READER: I now understand why the English hold India. I should like to know your views about the condition of our country.

EDITOR: It is a sad condition.[2] In thinking of it, my eyes water and my throat gets parched.[3] I have grave doubts whether I shall be able sufficiently to explain what is in my heart. It is my deliberate opinion that India is being ground down not under the English heel but[4] under that of modern civilisation. It is groaning under the monster's terrible weight. There is yet time to escape it, but every day makes it more and more difficult. Religion is dear to me, and[5] my first complaint is that India is becoming irreligious. Here, I am not thinking of the Hindu, the Mahomedan, or the Zoroastrian religion, but of that religion which underlies all religions. We are turning away from God.

READER: How so?

EDITOR: There is a charge laid against us that we are a lazy people, and[6] that the Europeans are industrious and enterprising. We have accepted the charge and we, therefore, wish[7] to change our condition. Hinduism, Islamism,[8] Zoroastrianism, Christianity and all other religions teach that we should remain passive about worldly pursuits and active about godly pursuits, that we should set a limit to our worldly ambition, and[9] that our religious ambition should be illimitable. Our activity should be directed into the latter channel.

READER: You seem to be encouraging religious charlatanism. Many a cheat has by talking in a similar strain led[10] the people astray.

EDITOR: You are bringing an unlawful charge against religion. Humbug there undoubtedly is about all religions. Where there is light, there is also shadow. I am prepared to maintain that humbugs in worldly matters are far worse than the humbugs in religion. The humbug of civilisation that I endeavour to show to you[11] is not to be found in religion.

READER: How can you say that? In the name of religion Hindus and Mahomedans fought against one another. For the same cause, Christians fought Christians. Thousands of innocent men have been murdered, thousands have been burned and tortured in its name. Surely, this is much worse than any civilisation.

EDITOR: I certainly submit that the above hardships are far more bearable than those of civilisation. Everybody understands that the cruelties you have named are not part of religion, although[12] they have been practised in its name; therefore, there is no aftermath to these cruelties. They will always happen so long as there are to be found ignorant and credulous people. But there is no end to the victims destroyed in the fire of civilisation. Its deadly effect is that people come under its scorching flames believing it to be all good. They become utterly irreligious and, in reality, derive little advantage from the world. Civilisation is like a mouse gnawing while it is soothing us. When its full effect is realised, we will see that religious superstition is harmless compared to that of modern civilisation. I am not pleading for a continuance of religious superstitions. We will certainly fight them tooth and nail, but we can never do so by disregarding religion.[13] We can only do so by appreciating and conserving the latter.

READER: Then you will contend that the *Pax Britannica*[14] is a useless encumbrance?[15]

EDITOR: You may see peace if you like; I see none.

READER: You make light of the terror that the Thugs, the Pindaris, the Bhils were to the country.

EDITOR: If you will give the matter some thought, you will see that the terror was by no means such a mighty thing. If it had been a very substantial thing, the other people would have died away before the English advent. Moreover, the present peace is only nominal, for by it we have become emasculated and cowardly. We are not to assume that the English have changed the nature of the Pindaris and the Bhils. It is, therefore, better to suffer the Pindari peril than that someone else should protect us from it, and thus render us effeminate. I should prefer to be killed by the arrow of a Bhil than to seek unmanly protection. India without such protection was an India full of valour. Macaulay[16] betrayed gross ignorance when he libelled Indians as being practically cowards. They never merited the charge. Cowards living in a country inhabited by hardy mountaineers, infested[17] by wolves and tigers must surely find an early grave. Have you ever visited our fields? I assure you that our agriculturists sleep fearlessly on their farms even to-day, and the English, you and I, would hesitate to sleep where they sleep.[18] Strength lies in absence of tear, not in the quantity of flesh and muscle we may have on our bodies. Moreover, I must remind you who desire Home Rule[19] that, after all, the Bhils, the Pindaris, the Assamese and the Thugs[20] are, our own countrymen. To conquer[21] them is your and my work. So long as we fear our own brethren, we are unfit to reach the goal.

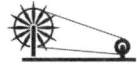

9

THE CONDITION OF INDIA
(CONTINUED) RAILWAYS[1]

READER: You have deprived me of the consolation[2] I used to have regarding peace in India.

EDITOR: I have merely given you my opinion on the religious aspect, but, when[3] I give you my views as to the poverty of India, you will perhaps begin to dislike me, because[4] what you and I have hitherto considered beneficial for India no longer appears to me to be so.

READER: What may that be?

EDITOR: Railways, lawyers and doctors have impoverished the country, so much so that,[5] if we do not wake up in time, we shall be ruined.

READER: I do now, indeed, fear that we are not likely to agree at all. You are attacking the very institutions which we have hitherto considered to be good.

EDITOR: It is necessary to exercise patience. The true inwardness of the evils of civilisation, you will understand with difficulty. Doctors assure us that a consumptive clings to life even when he is about to die. Consumption does not produce apparent hurt—it even produces a seductive colour about a patient's face, so as to induce the belief that all is well. Civilisation is such a disease, and we have to be very wary.

READER: Very well, then, I shall[6] hear you on the railways.

EDITOR: It must be manifest to you that, but for the railways, the English could not have such a hold on India as they have. The railways, too, have spread the bubonic plague. Without them, masses[7] could not move from place to place. They are the carriers of plague germs. Formerly we had natural segregation. Railways have also increased the frequency of famines, because, owing[8] to facility of means of locomotion, people sell out their grain, and it is sent to the dearest markets. People become careless, and so[9] the pressure of famine increases. They accentuate the evil nature of man. Bad men fulfil their evil designs with greater rapidity. The holy places of India have become unholy. Formerly, people went to these places with very great difficulty. Generally, therefore, only the real devotees visited such places. Nowadays, rogues[10] visit them in order to practise their roguery.

READER: You have given a one-sided account. Good men can visit these places as well as bad men. Why do they not take the fullest advantage of the railways?

EDITOR: Good travels at a snail's pace—it can, therefore, have little to do with the railways. Those who want to do good are not selfish, they are not in a hurry, they know that to impregnate people with good requires a long time. But evil has wings.

To build a house takes time. Its destruction takes none. So the railways can become a distributing agency for the evil one only. It may be a debatable matter whether railways spread famines, but it is beyond dispute that they propagate evil.

READER: Be that as it may, all the disadvantages of railways are more than counter balanced by the fact that it is due to them that we see in India the new spirit of nationalism.

EDITOR: I hold this to be a mistake. The English have taught us that we were not one nation before, and[11] that it will require centuries before we become one nation. This is without foundation. We were one nation before they came to India. One thought inspired us. Our mode of life was the same. It was because we were one nation that they were able to establish one kingdom. Subsequently, they divided us.

READER: This requires an explanation.

EDITOR: I do not wish to suggest that because we were one nation we had no differences, but it is submitted that our leading men travelled through-out India either on foot or in bullock-carts. They learned one another's languages, and there[12] was no aloofness between them. What do you think could have been the intention of those far-seeing[13] ancestors of ours who established Shevetbindu Rameshwar in the South, Juggernaut in the South-East,[14] and Hardwar in the North as places of pilgrimage? You will admit they were no fools. They knew that worship of God could have been performed just as well at home. They taught us that those whose hearts were aglow with righteousness had the Ganges in their own homes. But they saw that India was one undivided land so made by nature. They, therefore, argued that it must be one nation. Arguing thus, they established holy places in various parts of India, and fired the people with an idea of nationality in a manner unknown in other parts of the world. Any two Indians are one as no two English-men are.[15] Only you and I and others who consider ourselves civilised[16] and superior persons imagine that we are many nations. It was after the advent of railways that we began to believe in distinctions, and you are at liberty now to say that it is through the railways that we are beginning to abolish those distinctions. An opium-eater may argue the advantage of opium-eating from the fact that he began to understand the evil of the opium habit after having eaten it. I would ask you to consider well what I have said on the railways.

READER: I will gladly do so, but one question occurs to me even now. You have described to me the India of the pre-Mahomedan period, but now we have Mahomedans, Parsees and Christians. How can they be one nation? Hindus and Mahomedans are old enemies. Our very proverbs prove it.[17] Mahomedans turn to the West for worship, whilst Hindus turn to the East. The former look down on the Hindus as idolators. The Hindus worship the cow, the Mahomedans kill her. The Hindus believe in the doctrine of non-killing, the Mahomedans do not. We thus meet with differences at every step. How can India be one nation?

10

THE CONDITION OF INDIA (CONTINUED). THE HINDUS AND THE MAHOMEDANS[1]

EDITOR: Your last question is a serious one, and yet, on careful consideration, it will be found to be easy of solution. The question arises because of the presence of the railways, of the lawyers, and of the doctors. We shall presently examine the last two. We have already considered the railways. I should, however, like to add that man is so made by nature as require him to restrict his movements as far as to his hands and feet will take him. If we did not rush about from place to place by means of railways and such other maddening conveniences, much of the confusion that arises would be obviated. Our difficulties are of our own creation. God set a limit to a man's locomotive ambition in the construction of his body. Man immediately proceeded to discover means of overriding the limit. God gifted man with intellect that he might know his Maker. Man abused it, so[2] that he might forget his Maker. I am so constructed that I can only serve my immediate neighbours, but, in my conceit, I[3] pretend to have discovered that I must with my body serve every individual in the Universe. In thus attempting the impossible, man comes in contact with different natures, different religions, and is utterly confounded. According to this reasoning, it must be apparent to you that railways are a most dangerous institution. Man has therethrough gone further away from his Maker.[4]

READER: But I am impatient to hear your answer to my question. Has the introduction of Mahomedanism[5] not unmade the nation?

EDITOR: India cannot cease to be one nation because people belonging to different religions live in it. The introduction of foreigners does not necessarily destroy the nation, they[6] merge in it. A country is one nation only when such a condition obtains in it. That country must have a faculty for assimilation. India has ever been such a country. In reality, there are as many religions as there are individuals, but those who are conscious of the spirit of nationality do not interfere with one another's religion. If they do, they are not fit to be considered a nation. If the Hindus believe that India should be peopled only by Hindus, they are living in dreamland. The Hindus, the Mahomedans, the Parsees and the Christians who have made India their country are fellow-countrymen,[7] and they will have to live in unity if only[8] for their own interest. In no part of the world are one nationality and one religion synonymous terms: nor[9] has it ever been so in India.

READER: But what about the inborn enmity between Hindus and Mahonmedans?

EDITOR: That phrase has been invented by our mutual enemy. When the Hindus and Mahomedans fought against one another, they certainly spoke in that strain. They have long since ceased to fight. How, then, can there be any inborn enmity? Pray remember this too, that we did not cease to fight only after British occupation. The Hindus flourished under Moslem sovereigns, and[10] Moslems under the Hindu. Each party recognised that mutual fighting was suicidal, and that neither party would abandon its religion by force of arms. Both parties, therefore, decided to live in peace. With the English advent, the quarrels recommenced.[11]

The proverbs you have quoted were coined when both were fighting; to[12] quote them now is obviously harmful. Should we not remember that many Hindus and Mahomedans own the same ancestors, and the same blood runs through their veins? Do people become enemies because they change their religion? Is the God of the Mahomedan different from the God of the Hindu? Religions are different roads converging to the same point. What does it matter that we take different roads, so[13] long as we reach the same goal? Wherein is the cause for quarrelling?

Moreover, there are deadly proverbs as between the followers of Shiva and those of Vishnu, yet nobody suggests that these two do not belong to the same nation. It is said that the Vedic religion is different from Jainism, but[14] the followers of the respective faiths are not different nations. The fact is that we have become enslaved, and,[15] therefore, quarrel and like to have our quarrels decided by a third party. There are Hindu iconoclasts as there are Mahomedan. The more we advance in true knowledge, the better we shall understand that we need not be at war with those whose religion we may not follow.

READER: Now I would like to know your views about cow protection.[16]

EDITOR: I myself respect the cow, that is, I look upon her with affectionate reverence. The cow is the protector of India, because, it being an agricultural country, is dependent on the cow's progeny. She is a most useful animal in hundreds of ways.[17] Our Mahomedan brethren will admit this.

But, just as I respect the cow, so do I respect my fellow-men. A man is just as useful as a cow, no[18] matter whether he be a Mahomedan or a Hindu. Am I, then, to fight with or kill a Mahomedan in order to save a cow? In doing so, I would become an enemy as well of the cow as of the Mahomedan.[19] Therefore, the only method I know of protecting the cow is that I should approach my Mahomedan brother and urge him for the sake of the country to join me in protecting her. If he would not listen to me, I should let the cow go for the simple reason that the matter is beyond my ability. If I were overfull of pity for the cow, I should sacrifice my life to save her, but[20] not take my brother's. This, I hold, is the law of our religion.

When men become obstinate, it is a difficult thing. If I pull one way, my Moslem brother will pull another. If I put on a superior air, he will return the compliment.[21] If I bow to him gently, he will do it much more so, and, if[22] he does not, I shall not be considered to have done wrong in having bowed. When the Hindus became insistent, the killing of cows increased. In my opinion, cow-protection societies may be considered cow-killing societies. It is a disgrace to us that we should need such societies. When we forgot how to protect cows, I suppose we needed such societies.

What am I to do when a blood-brother[23] is on the point of killing a cow? Am I to kill him, or to fall down at his feet and implore him? If you admit that I should adopt the latter course, I must do the same to my Moslem brother.

Who protects the cow from destruction by Hindus when they cruelly ill-treat her? Whoever[24] reasons with the Hindus when they mercilessly belabour the progeny of the cow with their sticks? But this has not prevented us from remaining one nation.

Lastly, if it be true that the Hindus believe in the doctrine of non-killing and the Mahomedans do not, what, I pray, is the duty of the former?[25] It is not written that a follower of the religion of Ahinsa[26] (non-killing) may kill a fellow-man. For him the way is straight. In order to save one being, he may not kill another. He can only plead—therein lies his sole duty.

But does every Hindu believe in Ahinsa?[27] Going to the root of the matter, not one man really practises such a religion, because we do destroy life. We are said to follow that religion because we want to obtain freedom from liability to kill any kind of life. Generally speaking, we may observe that many Hindus partake of meat and are not, therefore, followers of Ahinsa.[28] It is, therefore, preposterous to suggest that the two cannot live together amicably because the Hindus believe in Ahinsa[29] and the Mahomedans do not.

These thoughts are put into our minds by selfish and false religious teachers[30]. The English put the finishing touch. They a have habit of writing history; they[31] pretend to study the manners and customs of all peoples. God has given us a limited mental capacity, but they usurp the function of the God-head and indulge in novel experiments. They write about their own researches in most laudatory terms and hypnotise us into believing them. We, in our ignorance, then fall at their feet.[32]

Those who do not wish to misunderstand things may read up the Koran, and will find therein hundreds of passages acceptable to the Hindus; and the Bhagavad-Gita[33] contains passages to which not a Mahomedan can take exception.[34] Am I to dislike a Mahomedan because there are passages in the Koran I do not understand or like? It takes two to make a quarrel. If I do not want to quarrel with a Mahomedan, the latter will be powerless to foist a quarrel on me, and, similarly,[35] I should be powerless if a Mahomedan refuses his assistance to quarrel with me. An arm striking the air will become disjointed. If everyone will try to understand the core of his own religion and adhere to it, and will not allow false teachers to dictate to him, there will be no room left for quarrelling.

READER: But will the English ever allow the two bodies to join hands?

EDITOR: This question arises out of your timidity. It betrays our shallowness. If two brothers want to live in peace, is it possible for a third party to separate them? If they were to listen to evil counsels, we[36] would consider them to be foolish. Similarly, we Hindus and Mahomedans would have to blame our folly rather than the English, if we allowed them to put us asunder. A clay-pot[37] would break through impact; if not with one stone, then with another. The way to save the pot is not to keep it away from the danger point,[38] but to bake it so that no stone would break it. We have then to make our hearts of perfectly baked clay. Then we shall be steeled against all danger. This can be easily done by the Hindus. They are superior in numbers, they pretend that they are more educated,[39] they are, therefore, better able to shield themselves from attack on their amicable relations with the Mahomedans.

There is mutual distrust between the two communities. The Mahomedans, therefore, ask for certain concessions from Lord Morley. Why should the Hindus oppose this? If the Hindus desisted, the English would notice it, the Mahomedans would gradually begin to trust the Hindus, and brotherliness would be the outcome. We should be ashamed to take our quarrels to the English. Everyone can find out for himself that the Hindus can lose nothing by desisting. That man who has inspired confidence in another has never lost anything in this world.

I do not suggest that the Hindus and the Mahomedans will never fight. Two brothers living together often do so. We shall sometimes have our heads broken. Such a thing ought not to be necessary, but all men are not equiminded.[40] When people are in a rage, they do many foolish things. These we have to put up with. But, when[41] we do quarrel, we certainly do not want to engage counsel and to resort to English or any law-courts. Two men fight; both[42] have their heads broken, or one only. How shall a third party distribute justice amongst them? Those who fight may expect to be injured.

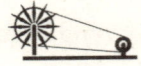

11

THE CONDITION OF INDIA (CONTINUED)
LAWYERS[1]

READER: You tell me that, when two men quarrel, they[2] should not go to a law-court. This is astonishing.

EDITOR: Whether you call it astonishing or not, it is the truth. And your question introduces us to the lawyers and the doctors. My firm opinion is that the lawyers have enslaved India, and they have accentuated the Hindu-Mahomedan dissensions, and have confirmed English authority.[3]

READER: It is easy enough to bring these charges, but it will be difficult for you to prove them. But for the lawyers, who would have shown us the road to independence? Who would have protected the poor? Who would have secured justice? For instance, the late Mr. Manomohan Ghose defended many a poor man free of charge.[4] The Congress, which you have praised so much, is dependent for its existence and activity upon the work of the lawyers. To denounce such an estimable class of men is to spell justice injustice, and you are abusing the liberty of the press by decrying lawyers.

EDITOR: At one time I used to think exactly like you. I have no desire to convince you that they have never done a single good thing. I honour Mr. Ghose's memory. It is quite true that he helped the poor. That the Congress owes the lawyers something is believable. Lawyers are also men, and there is something good in every man. Whenever instances of lawyers having done good can be brought forward, it will be found that the good is due to them as men rather than as lawyers. All I am concerned with is to show you that the profession teaches immorality; it is exposed to temptations from which few are saved.

The Hindus and the Mahomedans have quarrelled. An ordinary man will ask them to forget all about it, he[5] will tell them that both must be more or less at fault, and will advise them no longer to quarrel. They go to lawyers.[6] The latters' duty is to side with their clients, and to find out ways and arguments in favour of the clients to which they (the clients) are often strangers. If they do not do so, they[7] will be considered to have degraded their profession. The lawyers, therefore, will, as a rule, advance quarrels, instead of[8] repressing them. Moreover, men take up that profession, not in order to help others out of their miseries but to enrich themselves. It is one of the avenues of becoming wealthy, and their[9] interest exists in multiplying disputes. It is within my knowledge that they are glad when men have disputes. Petty pleaders actually manufacture them. Their touts, like so many leeches, suck the blood of the poor people. Lawyers are men who have little to do. Lazy people, in order to indulge in luxuries, take up such professions. This is a true statement. Any other argument is a mere pretension. It is the lawyers who have discovered that theirs is an honourable profession. They frame laws as they frame their own praises. They decide what fees they will charge, and[10] they put on so much side that poor people almost consider them to be heaven-born.

Why do they want more fees than common labourers? Why are their requirements greater ? In what way are they more profitable to the country than the labourers? Are those who do good entitled to greater payment? And, if they have done anything for the country for the sake of money, how shall it be counted as good?

Those who know anything of the Hindu-Mahomedan quarrels know that they have been often due to the intervention of lawyers. Some families have been ruined through them; they[11] have made brothers enemies. Principalities,[12] having come under lawyers'[13] power, have become loaded with debt. Many have been robbed of their all. Such instances can be multiplied.

But the greatest injury they have done to the country is that they have tightened the English grip. Do you think that it would be possible for the English to carry on their government[14] without law-courts? It is wrong to consider that courts are established for the benefit of the people. Those who want to perpetuate their power do so through the courts. If people were to settle their own quarrels, a third party would not be able to exercise any authority over them. Truly, men were less unmanly[15] when they settled their disputes either by fighting or by asking their relatives to decide upon[16] them. They became more unmanly and cowardly when they resorted to the courts of law. It was certainly a sign of savagery when they settled their disputes by fighting. Is it any the less so if[17] I ask a third party to decide between you and me? Surely, the decision of a third party is not always right. The parties alone know who is right. We, in our simplicity and ignorance, imagine that a stranger, by taking our money, gives us justice.

The chief thing, however, to be remembered is that, without lawyers, courts could not have been established or conducted, and[18] without the latter, the English could not rule. Supposing that there were only English judges, English pleaders and English police, they could only rule over the English. The English could not do without Indian judges and Indian pleaders. How the pleaders were made in the first instance and how they were favoured you should understand well. Then you will have the same abhorrence for the profession that I have. If pleaders were to abandon their profession and consider[19] it just as degrading as prostitution, English rule would break up in a day. They have been instrumental in having the charge laid against us that we love quarrels and courts, as fish love water. What I have said with reference to the pleaders necessarily applies to the judges; they are first cousins, and[20] the one gives strength to the other.

12

THE CONDITION OF INDIA (CONTINUED)[1]
DOCTORS

READER: I now understand the lawyers; the good they may have done I feel that is accidental. I feel that profession is certainly hateful.[2] You, however, drag in the doctors also, how is that?

EDITOR: The views I submit to you are those I have adopted. They are not original. Western writers have used stronger terms regarding both lawyers and doctors. One writer has likened the whole modern system to the Upas tree.[3] Its branches are represented by parasitical professions, including those of law and medicine, and over the trunk has been raised the axe of true religion. Immorality is the root of the tree. So you will see that the views do not come right out of my mind, but they represent[4] the combined experiences of many. I was at one time a great lover of the medical profession. It was my intention to become a doctor for the sake of the country. I no longer hold that opinion. I now understand why the medicine men (the vaids) among us have not occupied a very honourable status.

The English have certainly effectively used the medical profession for holding us. English physicians are known to have used the profession with several Asiatic potentates for political gain.

Doctors have almost unhinged us. Sometimes I think that quacks are better than highly qualified doctors. Let us consider: the business of a doctor is to take care of the body, or, properly speaking, not even that. Their business is really to rid the body of diseases that may afflict it. How do these diseases arise? Surely by our negligence or indulgence. I over-eat, I have indigestion, I go to a doctor, he gives me medicine, I am cured, I over-eat again, and I take his pills again. Had I not taken the pills in the first instance, I would have suffered the punishment deserved by me, and I would not have over-eaten again.[5] The doctor intervened and helped me to indulge myself. My body thereby certainly felt more at ease,[6] but my mind became weakened. A continuance of a course of a medicine must, therefore, result in loss of control over the mind.

I have indulged in vice, I contract a disease, a doctor cures me, the odds are that I shall repeat the vice. Had the doctor not intervened, nature would have done its work, and I would have acquired mastery over myself, would have been freed from vice, and[7] would have become happy.

Hospitals are institutions for propagating sin. Men take less care of their bodies, and[8] immorality increases. European doctors are the worst of all. For the sake of mistaken care of the human body, they kill annually thousands of animals. They practise vivisection. No religion sanctions this. All say that it is not necessary to take so many lives for the sake of our bodies.[9]

These doctors violate our religious instinct. Most of their medical preparations contain either animal fat or spirituous liquors; both of these are tabooed by Hindus and Mahomedans. We may pretend to be civilised, call religious prohibitions a superstition and wantonly indulge in what we like. The fact remains that the doctors induce us to indulge, and the result is that we have become deprived of self-control and have become effeminate. In these circumstances, we are unfit to serve the country. To study European medicine is to deepen our slavery.

It is worth considering why we take up the profession of medicine. It is certainly not taken up for the purpose of serving humanity. We become doctors so that we may obtain honours and riches. I have endeavoured to show that there is no real service of humanity in the profession, and that it is injurious to mankind. Doctors make a show of their knowledge, and charge exorbitant fees. Their preparations, which are intrinsically worth a few pennies, cost shillings.[10] The populace in[11] its credulity and in the hope of ridding itself of some disease, allows itself to be cheated. Are not quacks then, whom we know, better than the doctors who put on an air of humaneness?

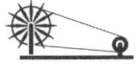

13

WHAT IS TRUE CIVILISATION?[1]

READER: You have denounced railways, lawyers and doctors. I can see that you will discard all machinery. What, then, is civilisation?

EDITOR: The answer to that question is not difficult. I believe that the civilisation India has evolved is not to be beaten in the world. Nothing can equal the seeds sown by our ancestors.[2] Rome went, Greece shared the same fate, the might of the Pharaohs was broken, Japan has become westernised, of China nothing can be said, but India is still, somehow or other, sound at the foundation.[3] The people of Europe learn their lessons from the writings of the men of Greece or Rome, which exist no longer in their former glory. In trying to learn from them, the Europeans imagine that they will avoid the mistakes of Greece and Rome. Such is their pitiable condition. In the midst of all this, India remains immovable, and that is her glory. It is a charge against India that her people are so uncivilised, ignorant and stolid, that it is not possible to induce them to adopt any changes. It is a charge really against our merit. What we have tested and found true on the anvil of experience, we dare not change. Many thrust their advice upon India, and she remains steady. This is her beauty; it[4] is the sheet-anchor of our hope.

Civilisation is that mode of conduct which points out to man the path of duty. Performance of duty and observance of morality are convertible terms. To observe morality is to attain mastery over our mind and our passions. So doing, we know ourselves. The Gujarati equivalent for civilisation means "good conduct".[5]

If this definition be correct, then India, as so many writers have shown, has nothing to learn from anybody else, and this is as it should be. We notice that mind is a restless bird; the more it gets the more it wants, and still remains unsatisfied. The more we indulge our passions, the[6] more unbridled they become. Our ancestors, therefore, set a limit to our indulgences. They saw that happiness was largely a mental condition. A man is not necessarily happy because he is rich, or unhappy because he is poor. The rich are often seen to be unhappy, the poor to be happy. Millions will always remain poor. Observing all this, our ancestors dissuaded us from luxuries and pleasures. We have managed with the same kind of plough as it existed[7] thousands of years ago. We have retained the same kind of cottages that we had in former times, and[8] our indigenous education remains the same as before. We have had no system of life-corroding competition. Each followed his own occupation or trade, and charged a regulation wage. It was not that we did not know how to invent machinery, but our forefathers knew that, if we set our hearts after such things, we would become slaves and lose our moral fibre. They therefore,[9] after due deliberation, decided that we should only do what we could with our hands and feet. They saw that our real happiness and health consisted in a proper use of our hands and feet. They further reasoned that large cities were a snare and a useless incumbrance, and that people would not be happy in them, that there would be gangs of thieves and robbers, prostitution and vice flourishing in them, and that poor men would be robbed by rich men.[10] They were, therefore, satisfied with small villages. They saw that kings and their swords were inferior to the sword of ethics, and they, therefore, held the sovereigns of the earth to be inferior to the Rishis and the Fakirs. A nation with a constitution like this is fitter to teach others than to learn from others. This nation had courts, lawyers and doctors, but they were all within bounds. Everybody knew that these professions were not particularly superior; moreover, these vakils and vaids did not rob people; they[11] were considered people's dependents, not their masters. Justice was tolerably fair. The ordinary rule was to avoid courts. There were no touts to lure people into them. This evil, too, was noticeable only in and around capitals. The common people lived independently, and[12] followed their agricultural occupation. They enjoyed true Home Rule.

And where this cursed modern civilisation has not reached, India remains as it was before. The inhabitants of that part of India will very properly laugh at your new-fangled notions. The English do not rule over them, nor will you ever rule over them. Those in whose name we speak we do not know, nor do they know us. I would certainly advise you and those like you who love the motherland to go into the interior that has yet not been polluted by the railways, and to[13] live there for six months; you might then be patriotic and speak of Home Rule.

Now you see what I consider to be real civilisation. Those who want to change conditions such as I have described are enemies of the country and are sinners.

READER: It would be all right if India were exactly as you have described it, but it is also India where there are hundreds of child widows, where two-year-old babies are married, where twelve-year-old girls are mothers and housewives, where women practise polyandry, where the practise of Niyog obtains, where, in the name of religion, girls dedicate themselves to prostitution, and where, in the name of religion, sheep and goats are killed.[14] Do you consider these also symbols of the civilisation that you have described?

EDITOR: You make a mistake. The defects that you have shown are defects. Nobody mistakes them for ancient civilisation. They remain in spite of it. Attempts have always been made, and will be made, to remove them.[15] We may utilise the new spirit that is born in us for purging ourselves of these evils. But what I have described to you as emblems of modern civilisation are accepted as such by its votaries. The Indian civilisation as described by me has[16] been so described by its votaries. In no part of the world, and under no civilisation, have all men attained perfection. The tendency of Indian civilisation is to elevate the moral being, that of the western civilisation is to propagate immorality.[17] The latter is godless, the former is based on a belief in God. So understanding and so believing, it behoves every lover of India to cling to the old Indian civilisation even as a child clings to its mother's breast.

14

HOW CAN INDIA BECOME FREE?[1]

READER: I appreciate your views about civilisation. I will have to think over them. I cannot take in all at once. What, then, holding the views you do, would you suggest for freeing India?

EDITOR: I do not expect my views to be accepted all of a sudden. My duty is to place them before readers like yourself. Time can be trusted to do the rest. We have already examined the conditions for freeing India, but we have done so indirectly; we[2] will now do so directly. It is a world-known maxim that the removal of the cause of a disease results in the removal of the disease itself. Similarly, if the cause of India's slavery be removed, India can become free.

READER: If Indian civilisation is, as you say, the best of all, how do you account for India's slavery?

EDITOR: This civilisation is unquestionably the best, but it is to be observed that all civilisations have been on their trial. That civilisation which is permanent outlives it. Because the sons of

India were found wanting, its civilisation has been placed in jeopardy. But its strength is to be seen in its ability to survive the shock. Moreover, the whole of India is not touched. Those alone who have been affected by western[3] civilisation have become enslaved. We measure the universe by our own miserable foot-rule. When we are slaves, we think that the whole universe is enslaved. Because we are in an abject condition, we think that the whole of India is in that condition. As a matter of fact, it is not so, but[4] it is as well to impute our slavery to the whole of India. But if we bear in mind the above fact, we can see that, if we become free, India is free. And in this thought, you have a definition of Swaraj. It is Swaraj when we learn to rule ourselves. It is, therefore, in the palm of our hands. Do not consider this Swaraj to be like a dream. Here there is no[5] idea of sitting still. The Swaraj that I wish to picture before you and me is such that, after we have once realised it, we will endeavour to the end of our lifetime to persuade others to do likewise. But such Swaraj has to be experienced by each one for himself.[6] One drowning man will never save another. Slaves ourselves, it would be a mere pretention to think of freeing others. Now you will have seen that it is not necessary for us to have as our goal the expulsion of the English. If the English become Indianised, we can accommodate them. If they wish to remain in India along with their civilisation, there is no room for them. It lies with us to bring about such a state of things.

READER: It is impossible that Englishmen should ever become Indianised.

EDITOR: To say that is equivalent to saying that the English have no humanity in them. And it is really beside the point whether they become so or not. If we keep our own house in order, only those who are fit to live in it will remain, others will leave of their own accord.[7] Such things occur within the experience of all of us.

READER: But it has not occurred in history.

EDITOR: To believe that what has not occurred in history will not occur at all is to argue disbelief in the dignity of man. At any rate, it behoves us to try what appeals to our reason. All countries are not similarly conditioned. The condition of India is unique. Its strength is immeasurable. We need not, therefore, refer to the history of other countries. I have drawn attention to the fact that, when other civilisations have succumbed, the Indian has survived many a shock.

READER: I cannot follow this. There seems little doubt that we shall have to expel the English by force of arms. So long as they are in the country, we cannot rest. One of our poets says that slaves cannot even dream of happiness.[8] We are day by day becoming weakened owing to the presence of the English. Our greatness is gone; our people look like terrified men. The English are in the country like a blight which we must remove by every means.

EDITOR:[9] In your excitement, you have forgotten all we have been considering. We brought the English, and we keep them. Why do you forget that our adoption of their civilisation makes their presence in India at all possible? Your hatred against them ought to be transferred to their civilisation. But let us assume that we have to drive away the English by fighting, how is that to be done?

READER: In the same way as Italy did it. What it was possible for Mazzini and Garibaldi to do, is possible for us.[10] You cannot deny that they were very great men.[11]

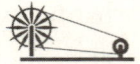

15

ITALY AND INDIA

EDITOR: It is well that you have instanced Italy. Mazzini[1] was a great and good man; Garibaldi[2] was a great warrior. Both are adorable; from their lives, we can learn much. But the condition of Italy was different from that of India. In the first instance, the difference between Mazzini and Garibaldi is worth noting. Mazzini's ambition was not, and has not yet been, realised regarding Italy.[3] Mazzini has shown in his writings on the duty of man that every man must learn how to rule himself.[4] This has not happened in Italy. Garibaldi did not hold this view of Mazzini's. Garibaldi gave, and every Italian took, arms. Italy and Austria had the same civilisation; they were cousins in this respect. It was a matter of tit for tat. Garibaldi simply wanted Italy to be free from the Austrian yoke. The machinations of Minister Cavour disgrace that portion of the history of Italy. And what has been the result? If you believe that, because, Italians rule Italy, the Italian nation is happy, you are groping in darkness.[5] Mazzini has shown conclusively that Italy did not become free. Victor Emanuel gave one meaning to the expression; Mazzini gave another. According to Emanuel, Cavour, and even Garibaldi, Italy meant the King of Italy and his henchmen. According to Mazzini, it meant the whole of the Italian people, that is, its agriculturists. Emanuel was only its servant. The Italy of Mazzini still remains in a state of slavery. At the time of the so-called national war, it was a game of chess between two rival kings, with the[6] people of Italy as pawns. The working classes in that land are still unhappy. They therefore,[7] indulge in assassination, rise in revolt, and rebellion on their part is always expected. What substantial gain did Italy obtain after the withdrawal of the Austrian troops? The gain was only nominal. The reforms for the sake of which the war was supposed to have been undertaken have not yet been granted. The condition of the people in general still remains the same. I am sure you do not wish to reproduce such a condition in India. I believe that you want the millions of India to be happy, not that you want the reins of Government in your hands. If that be so, we have to consider only one thing: how can the millions obtain self rule?[8] You will admit that people under several Indian princes are being ground down. The latter mercilessly crush them. Their tyranny is greater than that of the English; and, if you want[9] such tyranny in India, then we shall never agree. My patriotism does not teach me that I am to allow people to be crushed under the heel of Indian princes, if only[10] the English retire. If I have the power, I should resist the tyranny of Indian princes just as much as that of the English. By patriotism, I mean the welfare of the whole people, and, if I could secure it at the hands of the English, I should bow down my head to them. If any Englishman dedicated his life to securing the freedom of India, resisting tyranny and serving the land, I should welcome that Englishman as an Indian.

Again, India can fight like Italy only when she has arms. You have not considered this problem at all. The English are splendidly armed; that[11] does not frighten me, but it is clear that, to pit ourselves against them in arms, thousands of Indians must be armed. If such a thing be possible, how many years will it take? Moreover, to arm India on a large scale is to Europeanise it. Then her condition will be just as pitiable as that of Europe. This means, in short, that India must accept European civilisation, and, if that[12] is what we want, the best thing is that we have among us those who are so well trained in that civilisation. We will then fight for a few rights, will get what we can, and so[13] pass our days. But the fact is that the Indian nation will not adopt arms, and it is well that it does not.

READER: You are over-assuming facts. All need not be armed. At first, we will assassinate a few Englishmen and strike terror; then, a few men who will have been armed will fight openly. We may have to lose a quarter of a million men, more or less, but we will regain our land. We will undertake guerilla warfare, and defeat the English.[14]

EDITOR: That is to say, you want to make the holy land of India unholy. Do you not tremble to think of freeing India by assassination? What we need to do is to kill ourselves.[15] It is a cowardly thought that[16] of killing others. Whom do you suppose to free by assassination? The millions of India do not desire it. Those who are intoxicated by the wretched modern civilisation think these things. Those who will rise to power by murder will certainly not make the nation happy. Those who believe that India has gained by Dhingra's act and such other acts[17] in India make a serious mistake.

Dhingra was a patriot, but his love was blind. He gave his body in a wrong way; its ultimate result can only be mischievous.

READER: But you will admit that the English have been frightened by these murders, and that Lord Morley's reforms are due to fear.

EDITOR: The English are both a timid and a brave nation. She[18] is, I believe, easily influenced by the use of gunpowder. It is possible that Lord Morley has granted the reforms through fear, but what is granted under fear can be retained only so long as the fear lasts.

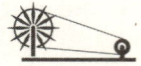

16

BRUTE-FORCE[1]

READER: This is a new doctrine: that[2] what is gained through fear is retained only while the fear lasts. Surely, what is given will not be withdrawn?

EDITOR: Not so. The Proclamation of 1857 was given at the end of a revolt, and for the purpose of preserving peace. When peace was secured and people became simple-minded, its[3] full effect was toned down. If I ceased stealing for fear of punishment, I would re-commence[4] the operation so soon as the fear is withdrawn from me. This is almost a universal experience. We have assumed that we can get men to do things by force and, therefore, we use force.

READER: Will you not admit that you are arguing against yourself? You know that what the English obtained in their own country they have obtained by using brute-force. I know you have argued that what they have obtained is useless, but that does not affect my argument. They wanted useless things, and they[5] got them. My point is that their desire was fulfilled. What does it matter what means they adopted? Why should we not obtain our goal, which is good, by any means whatsoever, even by using violence? Shall I think of the means when I have to deal with a thief in the house? My duty is to drive him out anyhow. You seem to admit that we have received nothing, and that we shall receive nothing by petitioning. Why, then, may we not do so by using brute-force? And, to retain what we may receive, we[6] shall keep up the fear by using the same force to the extent that it may be necessary. You will not find fault with a continuance of force to prevent a child from thrusting its foot into fire? Somehow or other, we[7] have to gain our end.

EDITOR: Your reasoning is plausible. It has deluded many. I have used similar arguments before now. But I think I know better now, and I shall endeavour to undeceive you. Let us first take the argument that we are justified in gaining our end by using brute-force, because the English gained theirs by using similar means. It is perfectly true that they used brute-force, and that it is possible for us to do likewise, but, by using similar means,[8] we can get only the same thing that they got. You will admit that we do not want that. Your belief that there is no connection between the means and the end is a great mistake. Through that mistake even men who have been considered religious have committed grievous crimes. Your reasoning is the same as saying that we can get a rose through planting a noxious weed. If I want to cross the ocean, I can do so only by means of a vessel; if I were to use a cart for that purpose, both the cart and I would soon find the bottom. "As is the God, so is the votary" is a maxim worth considering. Its meaning has been distorted, and men[9] have gone astray. The means may be likened to a seed, the end to a tree; and there is just the same inviolable connection between the means and the end as there is between the seed and the tree. I am not likely to obtain the result flowing from the worship of God by laying myself prostrate before Satan. If, therefore, anyone were to say: "I want to worship God, it[10] does not matter that I do so by means of Satan," it would be set down as ignorant folly. We reap exactly as we sow. The English in 1833 obtained greater voting power by violence. Did they by using brute-force better appreciate their duty? They wanted the right of voting, which they obtained by using physical force. But real rights are a result of performance of duty; these rights they have not obtained. We, therefore, have before us in England the farce of everybody wanting and insisting on his rights, nobody thinking of his duty. And, where everybody wants rights, who shall give them to whom? I do not wish to imply that they never perform their duty, but I do wish to imply that they do not perform the duty to which those rights should correspond; and, as they do not perform that particular duty, namely, acquire fitness, their rights have proved a burden to them.[11] In other words, what they have obtained is an exact result of the means they adopted. They used the means corresponding to the end. If I want to deprive you of your watch, I shall certainly have to fight for it; if I[12] want to buy your watch, I shall have to pay you for it; and, if I want a gift, I shall have to plead for it; and, according to the means I employ, the watch is stolen property, my own property, or a donation. Thus we see three different results from three different means. Will you still say that means do not matter?

Now we shall take the example given by you of the thief to be driven out. I do not agree with you that the thief may be driven out by any means. If it is my father who has come to steal, I shall use one kind of means. If it is an acquaintance, I shall use another, and, in the case of a perfect stranger, I shall use a third.[13] If it is a white man, you will perhaps say, you will[14] use means different from those you will adopt with an Indian thief. If it is a weakling, the means will be different from those to be adopted for dealing with an equal in physical strength; and, if the thief is armed from tip to toe,[15] I shall simply remain quiet. Thus we have a variety of means between the father and the armed man. Again, I fancy that I should pretend to be sleeping whether the thief was my father or that strong armed man. The reason for this is that my father would also be armed, and I[16] should succumb to the strength possessed by either, and allow my things to be stolen. The strength of my father would make me weep with pity; the strength of the armed man would rouse in me anger, and we[17] should become enemies. Such is the curious situation. From these examples, we may not be able to agree as to the means to be adopted in each case. I myself seem clearly to see what should be done in all these cases, but the remedy may frighten you. I, therefore, hesitate to[18] place it before you. For the time being, I[19] will leave you to guess it, and, if you cannot, it is clear that you will[20] have to adopt different means in each case. You will also have seen that any means will not avail to drive away the thief. You will have to adopt means to fit each case. Hence it follows that your duty is *not* to drive away the thief by any means you like.

Let us proceed a little further. That well-armed man has stolen your property, you have harboured the thought, you are filled with anger; you argue that you want to punish that rogue, not for your own sake, but for the good of your neighbours; you have collected a number of armed men, you want to take his house by assault, he is duly informed of it, he runs away; he, too, is incensed.[21] He collects his brother-robbers,[22] and sends you a defiant message that he will commit robbery in broad daylight.

You are strong, you do not fear him, you[23] are prepared to receive him. Meanwhile, the robber pesters your neighbours. They complain before you, you reply that you are doing all for their sake, you do not mind that your own goods have been stolen.[24] Your neighbours reply that the robber never pestered them before, and that he commenced his depredations only after you declared hostilities against him. You are between Scylla and Charybdis.[25] You are full of pity for the poor men. What they say is true. What are you to do? You will be disgraced if you now leave the robber alone. You, therefore, tell the poor men: "Never mind. Come, my wealth is yours, I will give you arms, I will teach you how to use them; you should belabour the rogue; don't you leave him alone." And so the battle grows; the[26] robbers increase in numbers; your neighbours have deliberately put themselves to inconvenience. Thus the result of wanting to take revenge upon the robber is that you have disturbed your own peace; you are in perpetual fear of being robbed and assaulted; your courage has given place to cowardice. If you will patiently examine the argument, you will see that I have not overdrawn the picture. This is one of the means. Now let us examine the other. You set this armed robber down as an ignorant brother; you intend to reason with him at a suitable opportunity; you argue[27] that he is, after all, a fellow-man; you[28] do not know what prompted him to steal. You, therefore, decide that, when you can, you will destroy the man's motive for stealing. Whilst you are thus reasoning with yourself, the man comes again to steal. Instead of being angry with him, you take pity on him. You think that this stealing habit must be a disease with him. Henceforth, you, therefore, keep your doors and windows open; you[29] change your sleeping-place, and you keep your things in a manner most accessible to him. The robber comes again, and is confused, as all this is new to him;[30] nevertheless, he takes away your things. But his mind is agitated. He inquires about you in the village, he comes to learn about your broad and loving heart, he repents, he begs your pardon, returns you your things, and leaves off the stealing habit. He becomes your servant, and you find for him honourable employment. This is the second method. Thus, you see different means[31] have brought about totally different results. I do not wish to deduce from this that all robbers will act in the above manner, or that all will have the same pity and love like you, but I wish only to show that only fair means can produce fair results, and that, at least in the majority of cases, if not, indeed, in all, the force of love and pity is infinitely greater than the force of arms.[32] There is harm in the exercise of brute-force, never in that of pity.

Now we will take the question of petitioning. It is a fact beyond dispute that a petition, without the backing of force, is useless. However, the late Justice Ranade used to say that petitions served a useful purpose because they were a means of educating people. They give the latter an idea of their condition, and warn[33] the rulers. From this point of view, they are not altogether useless. A petition of an equal is a sign of courtesy; a petition from a slave is a symbol of his slavery. A petition backed by force is a petition from an equal and, when he transmits his demand in the form of a petition, it testifies to his nobility. Two kinds of force can back petitions. "We will hurt[34] you if you do not give this" is one kind of force; it is the force of arms, whose evil results we have already examined. The second kind of force can thus be stated: "If you do not concede our demand, we will be no longer[35] your petitioners. You can govern us only so long as we remain the governed; we shall no longer have any dealings with you." The force implied in this may be described as love-force, soul-force or, more popularly but less accurately, passive resistance.[36] This force is indestructible. He who uses it perfectly understands his position. We have an ancient proverb which literally means: "One negative cures thirty-six diseases."[37] The force of arms is powerless when matched against the force of love or the soul.

Now we shall take your last illustration, that of the child thrusting its foot into fire. It will not avail you. What do you really do to the child? Supposing that it can exert so much physical force that it renders you powerless and rushes into fire, then you cannot prevent it. There are only two remedies open to you—either you must kill it in order to prevent it from perishing in the flames, or you must give your own life, because[38] you do not wish to see it perish before your very eyes. You will not kill it. If your heart is not quite full pity, it is possible that you will not surrender yourself by preceding the child and going into the fire yourself. You, therefore, helplessly allow it to go into the flames. Thus, at any rate, you are not using physical force. I hope you will not consider that it is still physical force, though of a low order, when you would forcibly prevent the child from rushing towards the fire if you could. That force is of a different order, and we have to understand what it is.

Remember that, in thus preventing the child, you are minding entirely its own interest, you are exercising authority for its sole benefit. Your example does not apply to the English. In using brute-force against the English, you consult entirely your own, that is, the national interest.[39] There is no question here either of pity or of love. If you say that the actions of the English, being evil, represent fire, and that they proceed to their actions through ignorance, and that, therefore, they occupy the position of a child, and that you want to protect such a child, then you will have to overtake every such evil action by whomsoever committed, and, as in the case of the child, you will have to sacrifice yourself.[40] If you are capable of such immeasurable pity, I wish you well in its exercise.

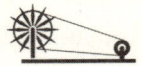

17

PASSIVE RESISTANCE[1]

READER: Is there any historical evidence as to the success of what you have called soul-force or truth-force? No instance seems to have happened of any nation having risen through soul-force. I still think that the evil-doers will not cease doing evil without physical punishment.

EDITOR: The poet Tulsidas has said aid "Of religion, pity or love is[2] the root, as egotism of the body. Therefore, we should not abandon pity so long as we are alive."[3] This appears to me to be a scientific truth. I believe in it as much as I believe in two and two being four. The force of love is the same as the force of the soul or truth. We have evidence of its working at every step. The universe would disappear without the existence of that force. But you ask for historical evidence. It is, therefore, necessary to know what history means. The Gujarati equivalent means: "It so happened." If that is the meaning of history, it is possible to give copious evidence. But, if it means the doings of kings and emperors, there can be no evidence of soul-force or passive resistance in such history. You cannot expect silver-ore in a tin-mine.[4] History, as we know it, is a record of the wars of the world, and so there is a proverb among Englishmen that a nation which has no history, that is, no wars, is a happy nation. How kings played, how they became enemies of one another, and[5] how they murdered one another is found accurately recorded in history, and, if this were[6] all that had happened in the world, it would have been ended long ago. If the story of the universe had commenced with wars, not a man would have been found alive to-day. Those people who have been warred against have disappeared, as, for instance, the natives of Australia, of whom[7] hardly a man was left alive by the intruders. Mark, please, that these natives did not use soul-force in self-defence, and it does not require much foresight to know that the Australians will share the same fate as their victims. "Those that wield[8] the sword shall perish by the sword." With us, the proverb is that professional swimmers will find a watery grave.

The fact that there are so many men still alive in the world shows that it is based not on the force of arms but on the force of truth or love. Therefore, the greatest and most unimpeachable evidence of the success of this force is to be found in the fact that, in spite of the wars of the world, it still lives on.

Thousands, indeed, tens of thousands, depend for their existence on a very active working of this force. Little quarrels of millions of families in their daily lives disappear before the exercise of this force. Hundreds of nations live in peace. History does not, and cannot, take note of this fact.[9] History is really a record of every interruption of the even working of the force of love or of the soul. Two brothers quarrel; one of them repents and re-awakens the love that was lying dormant in him; the two again begin to live in peace; nobody takes note of this. But, if the two brothers,[10] through the intervention of solicitors or some other reason, take up arms or go to law—which is another form of the exhibition of brute-force—their doings would be immediately noticed in the press, they would be the talk of their neighbours, and would probably go down to history. And what is true of families and communities is true of nations. There is no reason to believe that there is one law for families, and another for[11] nations. History, then, is a record of an interruption of the course of nature. Soul-force, being natural, is not noted in history.[12]

READER: According to what you say, it is plain that instances of this kind of passive resistance are not to be found in history. It is necessary to understand this passive resistance more fully. It will be better, therefore, if you enlarge upon it.

EDITOR: Passive resistance is a method of securing rights by personal suffering; it[13] is the reverse of resistance by arms. When I refuse to do a thing that is repugnant to my conscience, I use soul-force. For instance, the government of the day has passed a law which is applicable to me. I do not like it. If, by using violence, I[14] force the government to repeal the law, I am employing what may be termed body-force.[15] If I do not obey the law, and[16] accept the penalty for its breach, I use soul-force. It involves sacrifice of self.

Everybody admits that sacrifice of self is infinitely superior to sacrifice of others. Moreover, if this kind of force is used in a cause that is unjust, only the person using it suffers. He does not make others suffer for his mistakes. Men have before now done many things which were subsequently found to have been wrong. No man can claim to be absolutely in the right, or that a particular thing is wrong, because he thinks so, but it is wrong for him so long as that is his deliberate judgment. It is, therefore, meet[17] that he should not do that which he knows to be wrong, and suffer the consequence whatever it may be. This is the key to the use of soul-force.

READER: You would then disregard laws—this is rank disloyalty. We have always been considered a law-abiding nation. You seem to be going even beyond the extremists. They say that we must obey the laws that have been passed, but that, if the laws be bad, we must drive out the law-givers even by force.

EDITOR: Whether I go beyond them or whether I do not is a matter of no consequence to either of us. We simply want to find out what is right, and[18] to act accordingly. The real meaning of the statement that we are a law-abiding nation is that we are passive resisters. When we do not like certain laws, we do not break the heads of law-givers, but[19] we suffer and do not submit to the laws. That we should obey laws whether good or bad is a new-fangled notion. There was no such thing in former days. The people disregarded those laws they did not like, and suffered the penalties for their breach. It is contrary to our manhood, if we obey laws repugnant to our conscience. Such teaching is opposed to religion, and[20] means slavery. If the government were to ask us to go about without any clothing, should we do so? If I were a passive resister,[21] I would say to them that I would have nothing to do with their law. But we have so forgotten ourselves and become so compliant, that[22] we do not mind any degrading law.

A man who has realised his manhood,[23] who fears only God, will fear no-one[24] else. Man-made laws are not necessarily binding on him. Even the government do not expect any such thing from us. They do not say: "You must do such and such a thing," but they say: "If you do not do it, we will punish you." We are sunk so low, that we fancy[25] that it is our duty and our religion to do what the law lays down. If man will only realise that it is unmanly to obey laws that are unjust, no man's tyranny will enslave him. This is the key to self-rule or home-rule.

It is a superstition and an ungodly[26] thing to believe that an act of a majority binds a minority. Many examples can be given in which acts of majorities will be found to have been wrong, and[27] those of minorities to have been right. All reforms owe their origin to the initiation of minorities in opposition to majorities. If among a band of robbers, a knowledge[28] of robbing is obligatory, is a pious man to accept the obligation? So long as the superstition that men should obey unjust laws exists, so long will their slavery exist. And a passive resister alone can remove such a superstition.

To use brute-force,[29] to use gun-powder[30] is[31] contrary to passive resistance, for it means that we want our opponent to do by force that which we desire but he does not. And, if such a use of force is justifiable, surely he is entitled to do likewise by us. And so we should never come to an agreement. We may simply fancy, like the blind horse moving in a circle round a mill, that we are making progress. Those who believe that they are not bound to obey laws which are repugnant to their conscience have only the remedy of passive resistance open to them. Any other must lead to disaster.

READER: From what you say, I deduce that passive resistance is a splendid weapon of the weak, but that, when they are strong, they may take up arms.[32]

EDITOR: This is gross ignorance. Passive resistance, that is, soul-force, is matchless. It is superior to the force of arms.

How, then, can it be considered only a weapon of the weak? Physical-force men are strangers to the courage that is requisite in a passive resister. Do you believe that a coward can ever disobey a law that he dislikes? Extremists are considered to be advocates of brute-force. Why do they, then, talk about obeying laws? I do not blame them. They can say nothing else. When they succeed in driving out the English, and[33] they themselves become governors, they will want you and me to obey their laws. And that is a fitting thing for their constitution. But a passive resister will say he will not obey a law that is against his conscience, even though he may be blown to pieces at the mouth of a cannon.

What do you think? Wherein is courage required—in blowing others to pieces from behind a cannon or with a smiling face to approach a cannon and to be blown to pieces? Who is the true warrior—he who keeps death always as a bosom-friend or he[34] who controls the death of others? Believe me that a man devoid of courage and manhood[35] can never be a passive resister.

This, however, I will admit: that even a man weak in body is capable of offering this resistance. One man can offer it just as well as millions. Both men and women can indulge in it. It does not require the training of an army; it needs no Jiu-jitsu.[36] Control over the mind is alone necessary, and, when[37] that is attained, man is free like the king of the forest, and his very glance withers the enemy.

Passive resistance is an all-sided sword; it can be used anyhow; it[38] blesses him who uses it and him against whom it is used. Without drawing a drop of blood, it[39] produces far-reaching results. It never rusts, and[40] cannot be stolen. Competition between passive resisters does not exhaust. The sword of passive resistance does not require a scabbard. It is strange indeed that you should consider such a weapon to be a weapon merely of the weak.

READER: You have said that passive resistance is a speciality of India. Have cannons never been used in India?

EDITOR: Evidently, in your opinion, India means its few princes. To me, it means its teeming millions, on whom depends the existence of its princes and our own.[41]

Kings will always use their kingly weapons. To use force is bred in them. They want to command, but those who have to obey commands, do not want guns; and[42] these are in a majority throughout the world. They have to learn either body-force or soul-force. Where they learn the former, both the rulers and the ruled become like so many mad men[43], but, where they learn soul-force, the commands of the rulers do not go beyond the point of their swords, for true men disregard unjust commands. Peasants have never been subdued by the sword, and never will be. They do not know the use of the sword, and they are not frightened by the use of it by others. That nation is great which rests its head upon death as its pillow. Those who defy death are free from all fear. For those who are labouring under the delusive charms of brute-force, this picture is not over-drawn. The fact is that, in India, the nation at large has generally used passive resistance in all departments of life. We cease to cooperate with our rulers when they displease us. This is passive resistance.

I remember an instance when, in a small principality,[44] the villagers[45] were offended by some command issued by the prince. The former immediately began vacating the village. The prince became nervous, apologised to his subjects and withdrew his command. Many such instances can be found in India. Real home rule is possible only where passive resistance is the guiding force of the people. Any other rule is foreign rule.[46]

READER: Then you will say that it is not at all necessary for us to train the body?

EDITOR: I will certainly not say any such thing. It is difficult to become a passive resister, unless the body is trained. As a rule, the mind, residing in a body that has become weakened by pampering, is also weak, and, where there is no strength of mind, there[47] can be no strength of soul. We will have to improve our physique by getting rid of infant marriages and luxurious living. If I were to ask a man having a shattered body to face a cannon's mouth, I would make of myself a laughing-stock.[48]

READER: From what you say, then, it would appear that it is not a small thing to become a passive resister, and, if that is so, I would like you to explain how a man may become a passive resister.[49]

EDITOR: To become a passive resister is easy enough, but it is also equally difficult. I have known a lad of fourteen years become a passive resister; I have known also sick people doing like-wise; and I have also known physically strong and otherwise happy people being unable to take up passive resistance. After a great deal of experience, it seems to me that those who want to become passive resisters for the service of the country have to observe perfect chastity, adopt poverty, fellow truth, and cultivate fearlessness.[50]

Chastity is one of the greatest disciplines without which the mind cannot attain requisite firmness. A man who is unchaste loses stamina, becomes emasculated and cowardly. He whose mind is given over to animal passions is not capable of any great effort. This can be proved by innumerable instances. What, then, is a married person to do, is[51] the question that arises naturally;[52] and yet it need not. When a husband and wife gratify the passions, it is no less an animal indulgence on that account. Such an indulgence, except for perpetuating the race, is strictly prohibited. But a passive resister has to avoid even that very limited indulgence, because[53] he can have no desire for progeny. A married man, therefore, can observe perfect chastity. This subject is not capable of being treated at greater length. Several questions arise: How is one to carry one's wife with one? What are her rights, and such other questions?[54] Yet those who wish to take part in a great work are bound to solve these puzzles.

Just as there is necessity for chastity, so is there for poverty. Pecuniary ambition and passive resistance cannot well go together. Those who have money are not expected to throw it away, but they are expected to be indifferent about it. They must be prepared to lose every penny rather than give up passive resistance.

Passive resistance has been described in the course of our discussion as truth-force. Truth, therefore, has necessarily to be followed, and[55] that at any cost. In this connection, academic questions such as whether a man may not lie in order to save a life, etc., arise, but these questions occur only to those who wish to justify lying. Those who want to follow truth every time are not placed in such a quandary, and, if they are, they are still saved from a false position.

Passive resistance cannot proceed a step without fearlessness. Those alone can follow the path of passive resistance who are free from fear, whether as to their possessions, false honour, their relatives, the government, bodily injuries, death.[56]

These observances are not to be abandoned in the belief that they are difficult. Nature has implanted in the human breast ability to cope with any difficulty or suffering that may come to man unprovoked. These qualities are worth having, even for those who do not wish to serve the country. Let there be no mistake as those who want to train themselves in the use of arms are also obliged to have these qualities more or less. Everybody does not become a warrior for the wish. A would-be warrior will have to observe chastity, and[57] to be satisfied with poverty as his lot. A warrior without fearlessness cannot be conceived of. It may be thought that he would not need to be exactly truthful, but that quality follows real fearlessness. When a man abandons truth, he does so owing to fear in some shape or form. The above four attributes, then, need not frighten anyone. It may be as well here to note that a physical-force man has to have many other useless qualities which a passive resister never needs. And you will find that whatever extra effort a swordsman needs is due to lack of fearlessness. If he is an embodiment of the latter, the sword will drop from his hand that very moment. He does not need its support. One who is free from hatred requires no sword. A man with a stick suddenly came face to face with a lion, and[58] instinctively raised his weapon in self-defence. The man saw that he had only prated about fearlessness when there was none in him. That moment he dropped the stick, and[59] found himself free from all fear.

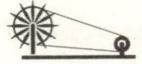

18

EDUCATION[1]

READER: In the whole of our discussion, you have not demonstrated the necessity for education; we[2] always complain of its absence among us. We notice a movement for compulsory education in our country. The Maharaja Gaekwar has introduced it in his territories. Every eye is directed towards them. We bless the Maharaja for it[3]. Is all this effort, then, of[4] no use?

EDITOR: If we consider our civilisation to be the highest, I have regretfully to say that much of the effort you have described is of no use. The motive of the Maharaja and other great leaders who have been working in this direction is perfectly pure. They, therefore, undoubtedly deserve great praise. But we cannot conceal from ourselves the result that is likely to flow from their effort.

What is the meaning of education? If it simply means a knowledge of letters, it is merely an instrument, and an instrument may be well used or abused.[5] The same instrument that may be used to cure a patient may be used to take his life, and so may a knowledge of letters. We daily observe that many men abuse it, and[6] very few make good use of it, and, if this is a correct statement, we have proved that more harm has been done by it than good.

The ordinary meaning of education is a knowledge of letters. To teach boys[7] reading, writing and arithmetic is called primary education. A peasant earns his bread honestly. He has ordinary knowledge of the world. He knows fairly well how he should behave towards his parents, his wife, his children and his fellow-villagers.[8] He understands and observes the rules of morality. But he cannot write his own name. What do you propose to do by giving him a knowledge of letters? Will you add an inch to his happiness? Do you wish to make him discontented with his cottage or his lot? And even if you want to do that, he will not need such an education. Carried away by the flood of western thought,[9] we[10] came to the conclusion, without weighing pros and cons, that we should give this kind of education to the people.

Now let us take higher education. I have learned Geography, Astronomy, Algebra, Geometry, etc. What of that? In what way have I benefited myself or those around me? Why have I learned these things? Professor Huxley has thus defined education:- "That man I think has had a liberal education who has been so trained in youth that his body is the ready servant of his will and does with ease and pleasure all the work that as a mechanism it is capable of; whose intellect is a clear, cold, logic engine with all its parts of equal strength and in smooth working order. ...whose mind is stored with a knowledge of the fundamental truths of nature... whose passions are trained to come to heel by a vigorous will, the servant of a tender conscience... who has learnt to hate all vileness and to respect others as himself. Such an one and no other, I conceive, has had a liberal education, for he is in harmony with Nature. He will make the best of her and she of him."[11]

If this be true education, I must emphatically say that the sciences I have enumerated above I have never been able to use for controlling my senses. Therefore, whether you take elementary education or higher education, it is not required for the main thing. It does not make of us men. It does not enable us to do our duty.

READER: If that is so, I shall have to ask you another question. What enables you to tell all these things to me? If you had not received higher education, how would you have been able to explain to me the things that you have?

EDITOR: You have spoken well. But my answer is simple: I do not for one moment believe that my life would have been wasted, had I not received higher or lower education. Nor do I consider that I necessarily serve because I speak. But I do desire to serve and, in endeavouring to fulfil that desire, I make use of the education I have received. And, if I am making good use of it, even then it is not for the millions, but I can use it only for such as you, and this supports my contention. Both you and I have come under the bane of what is mainly false education. I claim to have become free from its ill effects, and I am trying to give you the benefit of my experience, and, in doing so, I am demonstrating the rottenness of this education.[12]

Moreover, I have not run down a knowledge of letters under all circumstances. All I have shown is that we must not make of it a fetish. It is not our Kamdhuk. In its place it can be of use, and it[13] has its place when we have brought our senses under subjection, and put our ethics on a firm foundation.[14] And then, if we feel inclined to receive that education, we may make good use of it. As an ornament it is likely to sit well on us. It now follows that it is not necessary to make this education compulsory. Our ancient school-system is enough. Character-building has the first place in it, and[15] that is primary education. A building erected on that foundation will last.

READER: Do I then understand that you do not consider English education necessary for obtaining Home Rule?

EDITOR: My answer is yes and no. To give millions a knowledge of English is to enslave them. The foundation that Maucaulay[16] laid of education has enslaved us. I do not suggest that he had any such intention, but that has been the result. Is it not a sad commentary that we should have to speak of Home Rule in a foreign tongue?

And it is worthy of note that the systems which the Europeans have discarded are the systems in vogue among us. Their learned men continually make changes. We ignorantly adhere to their cast-off systems. They are trying, each division, to[17] improve its own status. Wales is a small portion of England. Great efforts are being made to revive a knowledge of Welsh among Welshmen. The English Chancellor, Mr. Lloyd George is[18] taking a leading part in the movement to make Welsh children speak Welsh. And what is our condition? We write to each other in faulty English, and from this even our M.A.'S are not free; our best thoughts are expressed in English; the proceedings of our Congress are conducted in English; our best newspapers are printed in English. If this state of things continues for a long time, posterity will—it is my firm opinion-condemn and curse us.

It is worth noting that, by receiving English education, we have enslaved the nation. Hypocrisy, tyranny, etc., have increased; English-knowing Indians[19] have not hesitated to cheat and strike terror into the people. Now, if we are doing anything for the people at all, we are paying only a portion of the debt due to them.

Is it not a most painful thing that, if I want to go to a court of justice, I must employ the English language as a medium; that, when I become a barrister, I may not speak my mother-tongue,[20] and that someone else should have to translate to me from my own language? Is not this absolutely absurd? Is it not a sign of slavery? Am I to blame the English for it or myself? It is we, the English-knowing men,[21] that have enslaved India. The curse of the nation[22] will rest not upon the English but upon us.

I have told you that my answer to your last question is both yes and no. I have explained to you why it is yes. I shall now explain why it is no.

We are so much beset by the disease of civilisation, that we cannot altogether do without English education. Those who have already received it may make good use of it wherever necessary. In our dealings with the English people, in our dealings with our own people, when we can only correspond with them through that language, and for the purpose of knowing how much disgusted[23] they (the English) have themselves become with their civilisation, we may use or learn English, as the case may be. Those who have studied English will have to teach morality to their progeny through their mother-tongue, and to teach them another Indian language; but when they have grown up, they may learn English, the ultimate aim being that we should not need it. The object of making money thereby should be eschewed. Even in learning English to such a limited extent, we will have to consider what we should learn through it and what we should not. It will be necessary to know what sciences we should learn. A little thought should show you that immediately we cease to care for English degrees, the rulers will prick up their ears.

READER: Then what education shall we give?

EDITOR: This has been somewhat considered above, but we will consider it a little more. I think that we have to improve all our languages. What subjects we should learn through them need not be elaborated here. Those English books which are valuable we should translate into the various Indian languages. We should abandon the pretension of learning many sciences. Religious, that is ethical, education will occupy the first place. Every cultured Indian will know in addition to his own provincial language, if a Hindu, Sanskrit; if a Mahomedan, Arabic; if a Parsee, Persian; and all Hindi.[24] Some Hindus should know Arabic and Persian; some Mahomedans and Parsees, Sanskrit. Several Northerners and Westerners[25] should learn Tamil. A universal language for India should be Hindi, with the option of writing it in Persian or Nagri characters. In order that the Hindus and the Mahomedans may have closer relations, it is necessary to know both the characters. And, if we can do this, we can drive the English language out of the field in a short time. All this is necessary for us slaves.[26] Through our slavery the nation has been enslaved, and it will be free with our freedom.

READER: The question of religious education is very difficult.

EDITOR: Yet we cannot do without it. India will never be godless. Rank atheism cannot flourish in that land.[27] The task is indeed difficult. My head begins to turn as I think of religious education. Our religious teachers are hypocritical and selfish; they[28] will have to be approached. The Mullas, the Dasturs,[29] and the Brahmins hold the key in their hands, but, if[30] they will not have the good sense, the energy that we have derived from English education will have to be devoted to religious education. This is not very difficult. Only the fringe of the ocean has been polluted, and it[31] is those who are within the fringe who alone need cleansing.

We who come under this category can even cleanse ourselves, because[32] my remarks do not apply to the millions. In order to restore India to its pristine condition, we have to return it. In our own civilisation, there will naturally be progress, retrogression, reforms and reactions;[33] but one effort is required, and that is to drive out Western civilisation. All else will follow.

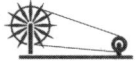

19

MACHINERY[1]

READER: When you speak of driving out Western civilisation, I suppose you will also say that we want no machinery.

EDITOR: By raising this question you[2] have opened the wound I had received. When I read Mr. Dutt's Economic History of India, I wept; and, as I think of it again, my heart sickens.[3] It is machinery that has impoverished India. It is difficult to measure the harm that Manchester has done to us.[4] It is due to Manchester that Indian handicraft has all but disappeared.

But I make a mistake. How can Manchester be blamed.[5] We wore Manchester cloth, and that is why Manchester wove it. I was delighted when I read about the bravery of Bengal. There are no cloth-mills[6] in that Presidency. They were, therefore, able to restore the original hand-weaving occupation. It is true, Bengal[7] encourages the mill-industry of Bombay. If Bengal had proclaimed a boycott of all machine-made goods, it would have been much better.

Machinery has begun to desolate Europe. Ruination is now knocking at the English gates. Machinery is the chief symbol of modern civilisation; it represents a great sin.

The workers in the mills of Bombay have become slaves. The condition of the women working in the mills is shocking. When there were no mills, these women were not starving. If the machinery craze grows in our country, it will become an unhappy hand. It may be considered a heresy, but I am bound to say that it were better for us to send money to Manchester and to use flimsy Manchester cloth, than[8] to multiply mills in India. By using Manchester cloth, we would only waste our money, but, by[9] reproducing Manchester in India, we shall keep our money at the price of our blood, because our very moral being will be sapped, and I call in support of my statement the very mill-hands as witnesses. And those who have amassed wealth out of factories are not likely to be better than other rich men. It would be folly to assume that an Indian Rockefeller would be better than the American Rockefeller.[10] Impoverished India can become free, but it will be hard for an India[11] made rich through immorality to regain its freedom. I fear we will have[12] to admit that moneyed men support British rule; their[13] interest is bound up with its stability. Money renders a man helpless. The other thing as harmful is sexual vice.[14] Both are poison. A snake-bite is a lesser poison than these two, because the former merely destroys the body, but[15] the latter destroy body, mind and soul. We need not, therefore, be pleased with the prospect of the growth of the mill-industry.

READER: Are the mills, then, to be closed down?

EDITOR: That is difficult. It is no easy task to do away with a thing that is established. We, therefore, say that the non-beginning of a thing is supreme wisdom. We cannot condemn mill-owners; we can but pity them. It would be too much to expect them to give up their mills, but we may implore them not to increase them. If they would be good, they would gradually contract their business. They can establish in thousands of households the ancient and sacred hand-looms, and[16] they can buy out the cloth that may be thus woven. Whether the mill-owners do this or not, people[17] can cease to use machine-made goods.

READER: You have so far spoken about machine-made cloth, but[18] there are innumerable machine-made things. We have either to import them or to introduce machinery into our country.

EDITOR: Indeed, our gods[19] even are made in Germany. What need, then, to speak of matches, pins and glassware? My answer can be only one. What did India do before these articles were introduced? Precisely the same should be done to-day. As long as we cannot make pins without machinery, so long will we do without them. The tinsel splendour of glassware we will have nothing to do with, and we will make wicks, as of old, with home-grown cotton, and use hand-made earthen saucers for lamps. So doing, we shall save our eyes and money, and will support Swadeshi, and so shall we attain Home Rule.[20]

It is not to be conceived that all men will do all these things at one time, or that some men will give up all machine-made things at once. But, if the thought is sound, we will always find out what we can give up, and will gradually cease to use this. What a few may do, others will copy, and the movement will grow like the cocoanut of the mathematical problem. What the leaders do, the populace will gladly follow. The matter is neither complicated nor difficult. You and I shall not wait until we can carry others with us. Those will be the losers who will not do it; and those who will not do it, although they appreciate the truth, will deserve to be called cowards.[21]

READER: What, then, of the tram-cars and electricity?

EDITOR: This question is now too late. It signifies nothing. If we are to do without the railways, we shall have to do without the tram-cars. Machinery is like a snake-hole which may contain from one to a hundred snakes. Where there is machinery there are large cities; and[22] where there are large cities, there are tram-cars and railways; and[23] there only does one see electric light. English villages do not boast[24] any of these things. Honest physicians will tell you that, where means of artificial locomotion have increased, the health of the people has suffered. I remember that, when in a European town there was a scarcity of money, the receipts of the tramway-company, of the lawyers and of the doctors, went down, and the people were less unhealthy.[25] I cannot recall a single good point in connection with machinery. Books can be written to demonstrate its evils.

READER: Is it a good point or a bad one that all you are saying will be printed through machinery?

EDITOR: This is one of those instances which demonstrate that sometimes poison is used to kill poison. This, then, will not be a good point regarding machinery. As it expires, the machinery, as it were, says to us: "Beware and avoid me. You will derive no benefit from me, and the benefit that may accrue from printing will avail only those who are infected with the machinery craze."[26] Do not, therefore, forget the main thing. It is necessary to realise that machinery is bad. We shall then be able gradually to do away with it. Nature has not provided any way whereby we may reach a desired goal all of a sudden. If, instead of welcoming machinery as a boon, we would look upon it as an evil, it would ultimately go.[27]

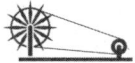

20

CONCLUSION[1]

READER: From your views I gather that you would form a third party. You are neither an extremist nor a moderate.

EDITOR: That is a mistake. I do not think of a third party at all. We do not all think alike. We cannot say that all the moderates hold identical views. And how can those who want to serve only, have a party?[2] I would serve both the moderates and the extremists. Where I should differ from them, I would respectfully place my position before them, and continue my service.[3]

READER: What, then, would you say to both the parties?

EDITOR: I would say to the extremists:- "I know that you want Home Rule for India; it is not to be had for your asking. Everyone will have to take it for himself. What others get for me is not Home Rule but foreign rule;[4] therefore, it would not be proper for you to say that you have obtained Home Rule, if you expelled the English.[5] I have already described the true nature of Home Rule. This you would never obtain by force of arms. Brute-force is not natural to the Indian soil.[6] You will have, therefore, to rely wholly on soul-force. You must not consider that violence is necessary at any stage for reaching our goal."

I would say to the moderates: "Mere petitioning is derogatory; we thereby confess inferiority. To say that British rule is indispensable is almost a denial of the Godhead. We cannot say that anybody or anything is indispensable except God. Moreover, common sense should tell us that to state that, for the time being, the presence of the English in India is a necessity, is to make them conceited.

"If the English vacated India bag[7] and baggage, it must not be supposed that she would be widowed. It is possible that those who are forced to observe peace under their pressure would fight after their withdrawal. There can be no advantage in suppressing an eruption; it must have its vent. If, therefore, before we can remain at peace, we must fight amongst ourselves, it is better that is no we do so. There is no occasion for a third party to protect the weak. It is this so called[8] protection which has unnerved us.

"Such protection can only make the weak weaker. Unless we realise this, we cannot have Home Rule. I would paraphrase the thought of an English divine and say that anarchy under home rule[9] were better than orderly foreign rule. Only, the meaning that the learned divine attached to home rule[10] is different to Indian Home Rule according to my conception. We have to learn, and to teach others, that we do not want the tyranny of either English rule or Indian rule."

If this idea were carried out, both the extremists and the moderates could join hands. There is no occasion to fear or distrust one another.

READER: What, then, would you say to the English?

EDITOR: To them I would respectfully say: "I admit you are my rulers. It is not necessary to debate the question whether you hold India by the sword or by my consent. I have no objection to your remaining in my country, but,[11] although you are the rulers, you will have to remain as servants of the people. It is not we who have to do as you wish, but it is you who have to do as we wish. You may keep the riches that you have drained away from this land, but you may not drain riches henceforth. Your function will be, if you so wish, to police India, you must abandon the idea of deriving any commercial benefit from us. We hold the civilisation that you support, to be the reverse of civilisation.[12] We consider our civilisation to be far superior to yours. If you realise this truth, it will be to your advantage; and, if[13] you do not, according to your own proverb, you should only live in our country in the same manner as we do. You must not do anything that is contrary to our religions. It is your duty as rulers that, for the sake of the Hindus, you should eschew beef, and for the sake of the Mahomedans, you should avoid bacon and ham.[14] We have hitherto said nothing, because[15] we have been cowed down, but you need not consider that you have not hurt our feelings by your conduct. We are not expressing our sentiments either through base selfishness or fear, but because it is our duty now to speak out boldly. We consider your schools and law courts to be useless. We want our own ancient schools and courts to be restored. The common language of India is not English but Hindi. You should, therefore, learn it. We can hold communication with you only in our national language.

"We cannot tolerate the idea of your spending money on railways and the military We see no occasion for either. You may fear Russia; we do not. When she comes we will look after her.

If you are with us, we will then receive her jointly. We do not need any European cloth. We will manage with articles produced and manufactured at home.[16] You may not keep one eye on Manchester, and the other on India. We can work together only if our interests are identical.

"This has not been said to you in arrogance. You have great military resources. Your naval power is matchless. If we wanted to fight with you on your own ground, we should be unable to do so; but, if[17] the above submissions be not acceptable to you, we cease to play the ruled. You may, if you like, cut us to pieces. You may shatter us at the cannon's mouth. If you act contrary to our will, we will not help you, and, without our help, we know that you cannot move one step forward.[18]

"It is likely that you will laugh at all this in the intoxication of your power. We may not be able to disillusion you at once, but, if[19] there be any manliness in us, you will see shortly that your intoxication is suicidal, and that your laugh at our expense is an aberration of intellect. We believe that, at heart, you belong to a religious nation.[20] We are living in a land which is the source of religions. How we came together need not be considered, but we can make mutual good use of our relations.

"You English who have come to India are not a good specimen of the English nation, nor can we, almost half-Anglicised Indians, be considered a good specimen of the real Indian nation.[21] If the English nation were to know all you have done, it would oppose many of your actions. The mass of the Indians have had few dealings with you. If you will abandon your so-called civilisation, and search into your own scriptures, you will find that our demands are just. Only on condition of our demands being fully satisfied may you remain in India, and, and if[22] you remain under those conditions, we shall learn several things from you, and you[23] will learn many from us. So doing, we[24] shall benefit each other and the world. But that will happen only when the root of our relationship is sunk in a religious soil."

READER: What will you say to the nation?

EDITOR: Who is the nation?

READER: For our purposes it is the nation that you and I have been thinking of, that is, those[25] of us who are affected by European civilisation, and[26] who are eager to have Home Rule.

EDITOR: To these, I would say: "It is only those Indians who are imbued with real love who will be able to speak to the English in the above strain without being frightened, and those only can be said to be so imbued who conscientiously believe that Indian civilisation is the best, and that European[27] is a nine day's wonder.[28] Such ephemeral civilisations have often come and gone, and will continue to do so. Those only can be considered to be so imbued, who, having experienced[29] the force of the soul within themselves, will not cower before brute-force, and will not, on any account, desire to use brute-force. Those only can be considered to have been so imbued who are intensely dissatisfied with the present pitiable condition, having already drunk the cup of poison.

If there be only one such Indian, he will speak as above to the English, and[30] the English will have to listen to him.

These demands are not demands, but they show our mental state. We will get nothing by asking; we shall have to take what we want, and we need the requisite strength for the effort, and[31] that strength will be available to him only who[32]

1. will only on rare occasions make use of the English language;[33]

2. if a lawyer, will give up his profession, and take up a hand-loom;[34]

3. if a lawyer, will devote his knowledge to enlightening both his people and the English;[35]

4. if a lawyer, will not meddle with the quarrels between parties, but will give up the courts and from his experience induce the people to do likewise;[36]

5. if a lawyer, will refuse to be a judge, as he will give up his profession;[37]

6. if a doctor, will give up medicine, and under-stand that, rather than mending bodies, he should mend souls;[38]

7. if a doctor, he will understand that, no matter to what religion he belong, it is better that bodies remain diseased rather than that they are cured through the instrumentality of the diabolical vivisection that is practised in European schools of medicine;[39]

8. although a doctor, will take up a hand-loom, and, if any patients come to him, will tell them the cause of their diseases, and will advise them to remove the cause rather than pamper them by giving useless drugs; he will understand that, if by not taking drugs, perchance the patient dies, the world will not come to grief, and that he will have been really merciful to him;[40]

9. although a wealthy man, regardless of his wealth, will speak out his mind and fear no one;[41]

10. if a wealthy man, will devote his money to establishing hand-looms, and encourage others to use hand-made goods by wearing them himself;[42]

11. like every other Indian, will know that this is a time for repentance, expiation and mourning;[43]

12. like every other Indian, will know that to blame the English is useless, that they came because of us, and remain also for the same reason, and that they will either go or change

their nature only when we reform ourselves;[44]

13. like others, will understand that, at a time of mourning, there can be no indulgence, and that, whilst we are in a fallen state, to be in gaol or in banishment is much the best;[45]

14. like others, will know that it is superstition to imagine it necessary that we should guard against being imprisoned in order that we may deal with the people;[46]

15. like others, will know that action is much better than speech; that it is our duty to say exactly what we think and face the consequences, and that it will be only then that we shall be able to impress anybody with our speech;[47]

16. like others, will understand that we will become free only through suffering;[48]

17. like others, will understand that deportation for life to the Andamans[49] is not enough expiation for the sin of encouraging European civilisation;[50]

18. like others, will know that no nation has risen without suffering; that, even in physical war-fare, the true test is suffering and not the killing of others, much more so in the warfare of passive resistance.[51]

19. like others, will know that it is an idle excuse to say that we will do a thing when the others also do it; that we should do what we know to be right, and that others will do it when they see the way; that, when I fancy a particular delicacy, I do not wait till others taste it; that to make a national effort and to suffer are in the nature of delicacies; and that to suffer under pressure is no suffering.[52]

READER: This is a large order. When will all carry it out?

EDITOR: You make a mistake. You and I have nothing to do with the others. Let each do his duty. If I do my duty, that is, serve myself, I shall be able to serve others. Before I leave you, I will take the liberty of repeating:

1. Real home-rule is self-rule or self-control.
2. The way to it is passive resistance: that is soul-force or love-force.
3. In order to exert this force, Swadeshi in every sense is necessary.
4. What we want to do should be done, not because we object to the English or that we want to retaliate, but[53] because it is our duty to do so. Thus, supposing that the English remove the salt-tax, restore our money, give the highest posts to Indians, withdraw the English troops, we shall certainly not use their machine-made goods, nor use the English language, nor many of their industries. It is worth noting that, these things are, in their nature, harmful; hence we do not want them. I bear no enmity towards the English, but I do towards their civilisation.

In my opinion, we have used the term "Swaraj" without understanding its real significance. I have endeavoured to explain it as I understand it, and my conscience testifies that my life henceforth is dedicated to its attainment.

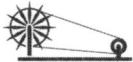

APPENDICES

SOME AUTHORITIES

The following books are recommended for perusal to follow up the study of the foregoing :-

"The Kingdom of God is Within You."-TOLSTOY.
"What is Art?"-TOLSTOY.
"The Slavery of Our Times."-TOLSTOY.
"The First Step."-TOLSTOY.
"How Shall We Escape?"-TOLSTOY.
"Letter to a Hindoo."-TOLSTOY.
"The White Slaves of England."-SHERARD.
"Civilisation[1], Its Cause and Cure." -CARPENTER.
"The Fallacy of Speed." -TAYLOR.
"A New Crusade." -BLOUNT.
"On the Duty of Civil Disobedience." -THOREAU.
"Life Without Principle." -THOREAU.
"Unto This Last."-RUSKIN.
"A Joy for Ever."-RUSKIN.
"Duties of Man."-MAZZINI.

"Defence and Death of Socrates."-From PLATO.

"Paradoxes of Civilisation^2."-MAX NORDAU.

"Poverty and Un-British Rule in India."-NAOROJI

"Economic History of India."-DUTT.

"Village Communities."-MAINE.

TESTIMONIES BY EMINENT MEN

The following extracts from Mr. Alfred Webb's valuable collection, if the testimony given therein be true, show that the ancient Indian civilisation has little to learn from the modern:-[1]

Victor Cousin (1792–1867)

Founder of Systematic Eclecticism in Philosophy[2]

"On the other hand, when we read with attention the poetical and philosophical movements of the East, above all, those of India, which are beginning to spread in Europe, we discover there so many truths, and truths so profound, and which make such a contrast with the meanness of the results at which the European genius has sometimes stopped, that we are constrained to bend the knee before that of the East, and to see in this cradle of the human race the native land of the highest philosophy."

J. Seymour Keay, M.P.

Banker in India and India Agent (Writing in 1883)[3]

"It cannot be too well understood that our position in India has never been in any degree that of civilians bringing civilisation to savage races. When we landed in India we found there a hoary civilisation, which during the progress of thousands of years had fitted itself into the character and adjusted itself to the wants of highly intellectual races. The civilisation was not perfunctory, but universal and all-pervading-furnishing the country not only with political systems, but with social and domestic institutions of the most ramified description. The beneficent nature of these institutions as a whole may be judged of from their effects on the character of the Hindu race. Perhaps there are no other people in the world who show so much in their characters the advantageous effects of their own civilisation. They are shrewd in business, acute in reasoning, thrifty, religious, sober, charitable, obedient to parents, reverential to old age, amiable, law-abiding, compassionate towards the helpless, and patient under suffering."

Friedrich Max Mueller, L.L.D.[4]

"If I were to ask myself from what literature we here in Europe, we who have been nurtured almost exclusively on the thoughts of Greeks and Romans, and of one Semitic race, the Jewish, may draw that corrective which is most wanted in order to make our inner lite more perfect, more comprehensive, more universal, in fact more truly human, a life, not for this life only, but a transfigured and eternal life-again I should point to India."

Michael G. Mulhall, F.R.S.S.

Statistics (1899)[5]

Prison population per 100,000 inhabitants:
Several European States 100 to 230
England and Wales 90
India 38

—"Dictionary of Statistics,"
Michael G. Mulhall, F.R.S.S. Routledge and Sons, 1899.

Colonel Thomas Munro

Thirty-two years' service in India[6]

"If a good system of agriculture, unrivalled manufacturing skill, a capacity to produce whatever can contribute to convenience or luxury; schools established in every village, for teaching reading, writing, and arithmetic; the general practice of hospitality and charity among each other; and above all a treatment of the female sex, full of confidence, respect and delicacy, are among the signs which denote a civilised people, then the Hindus are not inferior to the nations of Europe; and if civilisation is to become an article of trade between the two countries, I am convinced that this country [England] will gain by the import cargo."

Frederick von Schlegel[7]

"It cannot be denied that the early Indians possessed n knowledge of the true God; all their writings are replete with sentiments and expressions, noble, clear, and severely grand, as deeply conceived and reverently expressed as in any human language in which men have spoken of their God . . . Among nations possessing indigenous philosophy and meta. physics, together with an innate relish for these pursuits, such as at present characterises Germany, and, in olden times, was the proud distinction of Greece, Hindustan holds the first rank in point of time."

Sir William Wedderburn, Bart[8]

"The Indian village has thus for centuries remained a bulwark against political disorder, and the home of the simple domestic and social virtues. No wonder, therefore, that philosophers and historians have always dwelt lovingly on this ancient institution which is the natural social unit and the best type of rural life; self-contained, industrious, peace-loving, conservative in the best sense of the word . . . think you will agree with me that there is much that is both picturesque and attractive in this glimpse of social and domestic life in an Indian village. It is a harmless and happy form of human existence. Moreover, it is not without good practical outcome."

J. Young. Secretary

Sassoon Mechanics Institutés. (Within recent years.)[9]

"Those races, [the Indian] viewed from a moral aspect, are perhaps the most remarkable people in the world. They breath an atmosphere of moral purity, which cannot but excite admiration, and this is especially the case with the poorer classes, who, notwithstanding the privations of their humble lot, appear to be happy and contented. True children of nature, they live on from day to day, taking no thought of to. morrow, and thankful for the simple fare which Providence has provided for them. It is curious to witness the spectacle of coolies of both sexes returning home at night-fall after a hard day's work often lasting from sunrise to sunset. In spite of fatigue from the effects of the unremitting toil, they are for the most part gay and animated, conversing cheerfully together and occasionally breaking into snatches of light hearted song. Yet what awaits them on their return to the hovels which they call home? A dish of rice for food, and the floor for a bed. Domestic felicity appears to be the rule among the Natives, and this is the more strange when the customs of marriage are taken into account, parents arranging all such matters. Many Indian households afford examples of the married state in its highest degree of perfection. This may be due to the teachings of the Shastras, and to the strict injunctions which they inculcate with regard to marital obligations; but it is no exaggeration to say that husbands are generally devotedly attached to their wives, and in many instances the latter have the most exalted conception of their duties towards their husbands."

Abbe J. A. Dubois

Missionary in Mysore, Extracts from letter
dated Seringapatam, 15th December, 1820.[10]

"The authority of married women within their houses is chiefly exerted in preserving good order and peace among the persons who compose their families; and a great many among them discharge this important duty with a prudence and a discretion which have scarcely a parallel in Europe. I have known families composed of between thirty and forty persons, or more, consisting of grown sons and daughters, all married and all having children, living together under the superintendence of an old matron—their mother or mother-in-law. The latter, by good management, and by accommodating herself to the temper of the daughters-in-law, by using, according to circumstances, firmness or forbearance, succeeded in preserving peace and harmony during many years amongst so many females, who had all jarring interests, and still more jarring tempers. I ask you whether it would be possible to attain the same end, in the same circumstances, in our countries, where it is scarcely possible to make two women living under the same roof to agree together.

"In fact, there is perhaps no kind of honest employment in a civilised country in which the Hindu females have not a due share. Besides the management of the household, and the care of the family, which (as already noticed) under their control, the wives and daughters of husbandmen attend and assist their husbands and fathers in the labours of agriculture. Those of tradesmen assist theirs in carrying on their trade. Merchants are attended and assisted by theirs in their shops. Many females are shopkeepers on their own account; and without a knowledge of the alphabet or of the decimal scale, they keep by other means their accounts in excellent order. and are considered as still shrewder than the males themselves in their commercial dealings."

PRINTED BY THE INTERNATIONAL PRINTING PRESS,
PHOENIX, NATAL

AFTERWORD

Democracies are an excellent development in modern times. They disrupt the continuity of homogenous classes, castes, patriarchal norms, identity and race hegemony. They offer engagement to people hitherto denied all political, social and economic opportunities. This is a significant development. They also generate the notion of a "political self". People remain hopeful for continuous public engagement. Indeed, the spirit and the act of democracy should guide all engagements.

Yet, the democratic engagement has been limited to mobilization and did not expand to participation. Therefore, it could not overcome the "principle of (un)hearing". The principle of unhearing implies the ability of the institution to listen to only those who are a part of or proximately close to the institution. This closeness is denied in the mere politics of mobilization. In this framework, institutions and protocols precede people.

In contrast, Gandhi's framework of satyagraha and swaraj, when read in a hyphenated manner, provides a holistic meaning to people's participation. Satyagraha underscores the importance of people as sovereigns in achieving the interdependent political community of swaraj, which is based on the politics of participation.

The following two propositions become crucial to understanding this framework:

First, Gandhi's swaraj offers different notions of "political". Political is defined as a friend and enemy relation or the coexistence of permanent, perpetual or continuous conflict among people/groups. Swaraj offers a resolution of conflicts by way of satyagraha. Swaraj's political is not based on friend and enemy relations. It is also not a continuous conflict or just being aware of conflict. There is the resolution of conflict at the stage of satyagraha for the arrival of an interdependent political community. This understanding of Gandhi is crucial for moving beyond the Hobbesian framework, in which humans remain brutish or violent towards each other. This is not just a theoretical possibility, but is needed for "empirical hope", i.e. despite the existence of multiform of hatred, violence, exploitation and discrimination, humans can move beyond as they are not necessarily obsessed or violent, and they need an interdependent political community (which is the essence of Gandhi's swaraj).

Second, Gandhi also suggests that people-centric political community is paramount, in which norms of human beings are more robust than institutions' protocols. Over the centuries, institutions' protocols have become overpowering as guiding norms and assessments of people's hope and disappointment. Norms based on truth and non-violence make people sovereign against control. The interdependent political community offers permanency of people as sovereign against unjust formation.

In sum, for a participatory, people-centric political community, satyagraha for swaraj and swaraj for satyagraha is an existential imperative in contemporary times.

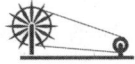

ACKNOWLEDGEMENTS

I am deeply grateful to Premanka Goswami, Penguin Random House India's editor, for suggesting that I work on *Hind Swaraj*. His unwavering interest and encouragement were instrumental in shaping my ideas, which had been evolving over a decade. His insistence on a fresh perspective for *Hind Swaraj* compelled me to align my own reflections in the introduction and notes. His unparalleled support and unwavering confidence were the driving force behind the completion of this book, and I have grown significantly from this experience.

I am grateful to the Central University of Gujarat for granting me leave to study, a crucial support that was instrumental in the book's development. My colleagues at the Department of Gandhian Thought and Peace Studies, particularly at the university in general, have extended all possible help numerous times. Students remained a critical component of this work.

The book was written during my visiting fellowship (2022–24) at the Centre for the Study of Developing Societies (CSDS), Delhi. The fellowship, in addition to seminars and formal discussions, provided opportunities for informal discussions during tea breaks and lunch, which greatly benefited me in revisiting some of the arguments. The contributions of my colleagues at the CSDS were not just forthcoming and encouraging, but they also formed the backbone of the book's completion. Awdhendra Sharan, director, CSDS, kept dialogically engaged to complete the book. I am thankful to Ananya Vajpeyi, Ashish Nandy, Awadhendra Sharan, Baidik Bhattacharya, Nishikant Kolge, Prabhat Kumar, Prathama Banerjee, Priyadarshini Vijaisri, Rajiv Bhargava, Rakesh Pandey, Ravi Sundaram, Ravikant, Sanjay Kumar and Sanjeer Alam. Preethi Nambiar and Praveen Rai provided all possible academic and administrative support at CSDS. I am grateful to them. Sachin, Ayodhya, Vikas, and the CSDS Library and its staff are equal companions in this process.

Post-publication of *Poorna Swaraj*, I immensely benefited from the reading, comments and discussions by teachers, colleagues, researchers and readers. Their engagement, not only on *Poorna Swaraj* but also on *Hind Swaraj,* concerning the difference, the idea of utopia, immediacy and integrity of Gandhian Philosophy, was invaluable. *Hind Swaraj* was invariably present in all readings, comments and discussions. I express my deep gratitude to readers, teachers, colleagues, friends, researchers, students and institutions who invited me to deliberations on Gandhi and *Poorna Swaraj*, of which *Hind Swaraj* was an undeniable component. Their collective support and camaraderie, as well as their intervention, were invaluable. Their names alphabetically are as follows: Abhay Prasad Singh, Akash Singh Thakur, Akhil Ranjan Datta, Amarendra Pandey, Anuradha Veeravalli, Aashish Xaxa, Awadhendra Sharan, Arka Chattopadhyay, Deepta Achar, Ghanshyam Shah, Harihar Bhattacharya, Hilal Ahmad, Ishwar Singh Dost, Indrajeet Jha, Jyotasana, Jyotsna Shree, Kamal Nayan Choubey, Lajwanti Chatani, Madhumita Sengupta, Mahendra

Parmar, Manas Kandi, Manindra Nath Thakur, Manoj Mohan, Manoj Rai, Madhulika Banerjee, Manoranjan Mohanty, Mayuri Jani, Mohammad Naushad, Narendra Singh, Naresh Goswami, Natasha Nongbri, Nishaant Choksi, Nupur Ray, Mritunjay, Om Prakash Dwivedi, P. Arun, Parimal Maya Sudhakar, Parvez Alam, Prabhat Kumar, Pravin Kumar, Praveen Verma, Prabhu Mahapatra, Prem Anand Mishra, Raman, Rama Shankar Singh, Ramchandra Pradhan, Ravikant, Rekha Saxena, Rityusha Mani Tiwary, Santosh Kumar Rai, Sanjeev Kumar, Satish Kumar Jha, Savita Singh, Saumya Gupta, Saurav Rai, Shivam Shandilya, Shreya Pandey, Smruti Ranjan Dhal, T. Longkoi Khiamniungan, Vandana Parmar, Vikas Gupta, Vikas Pathe, Vikram Singh Amarawat and Vivek Rai.

I am grateful to the following institutions for the invitation for interact on Gandhi and associated ideas, which gave me immense opportunity to interact with colleagues and students (alphabetically): Department of History and Gandhi Study Circle, Janaki Devi Memorial College, University of Delhi; Department of History, Gujarat Vidyapith, Ahmedabad; Department of History, University of Delhi; Department of History, Venkateshwara College, University of Delhi; Department of Political Science, University of Delhi; Department of Political Science, Aligarh Muslim University; Gandhi Study Circle, PGDAV College, University of Delhi; Gandhi Study Circle, Zakir Hussain College, University of Delhi; Department of Political Science, Kamala Nehru College, University of Delhi; Department of Political Science, St. Xavier College, Ranchi; Department of Sociology, Central University of Haryana; Department of Political Science and Gandhi Study Circle, Aryabhata College, University of Delhi; Dialogical Perspectives; Moturi Satyanarayana Centre for the Advance Study in the Humanities and Social Sciences, Krea University; Probhodha Trust, Kochi, Sree Sankara Vidyapeetom College, Valayanchirangara, Department of History, St. Peter's College, Kolenchery, and Department of Economics, Union Christian College, Aluva; *Nayi Parakh;* School of Government, MIT WPU, Pune; The Humanities and Social Sciences (HSS) IIT-Gandhinagar; School of Liberal Arts and Humanities, Bennett University; Sub Himalayan Research Institute, Purnia.

Aparna Abhijit (copy editor at PRHI) not only edited the book untiringly and enthusiastically but also helped clarify in multiple places. Her reasoning, arguments and coherent reading of the text led to the shape of the book. I am grateful to her for inviting attention to visible and invisible gaps in writing. For the book, she provided helpful comments, recommendations and edits. Aakriti Khurana designed the cover. Her creative sensitivity remains visible in this regard. It is a work of art, and I appreciate the effort put into it.

I am highly indebted to Aanya and Rityusha for generously treating my absence during the book's completion. My presence was almost equivalent to absence during this period. Rityusha's reading and comments helped to rearrange the arguments. I am thankful to her.

I remain responsible for errors or for unknowingly forgetting the names of many who participated in academic discussions with me.

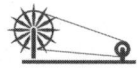

NOTES

Preface

1 This is peculiarly present in Dhananjay Keer's analysis. For him, *Hind Swaraj* responded to the arguments of Indian revolutionaries led by V.D. Savarkar (Keer, 1973, p. 168).

2 M.K. Gandhi, *Indian Home Rule* (Phoenix: International Printing Press, 1910), p. 103.

3 M.K. Gandhi, *Satyagraha in South Africa*, trans. Valji Govindji Desai (Madras: S. Ganesan, 1928), p. 354.

4 K. Raghavendra Rao, "The Political Theory in Hind Swaraj: A Preliminary Exploration", *Gandhi Marg* 1(7) (1979): 472.

5 Dennis Dalton, *Mahatma Gandhi: Non-violent Power in Action* (New York: Columbia University Press, 1993), p. 13.

6 Dennis Dalton, *Mahatma Gandhi: Non-violent Power in Action*, p. 13.

7 Dennis Dalton, *Mahatma Gandhi: Non-violent Power in Action*, p. 14.

8 Dennis Dalton, *Mahatma Gandhi: Non-violent Power in Action*, pp. 16–17.

9   Joan Valerie Bondurant, *Conquest of Violence: The Gandhian Philosophy of Conflict* (Princeton: Princeton University Press, 1988), p. 102.

10 R. R. Diwakar, *Satyagraha: Its Technique and History* (Bombay: Hind Kitabs, 1946), p. 2.

11 Gene Sharp, *Gandhi Wields the Moral Power* (Ahmedabad: Navajivan, 1960), p. 4.

12 Anthony J. Parel, "Introduction", in *M.K. Gandhi and Hind Swaraj and other writings,* ed. Anthony J. Parel (Cambridge: Cambridge University Press, 1997), p. xiii.

13 Rajeev Bhargava, "Introduction", in *Politics, Ethics and the Self: Re-Reading Gandhi's Hind Swaraj*, Rajeev Bhargava (New York: Routledge, 2022), p. 1.

14 Rudrangshu Mukherjee, "Gandhi's Swaraj", *Economic and Political Weekly 44*(50) (2009): 34.

15 David Arnold, *Gandhi: Profiles in Power* (Harlow: Longman, 2001), p. 66.

16 Anthony J. Parel, "Gandhi and the Emergence of the Modern Indian Political Canon", *The Review of Politics, 70*(1)(2008): 52.

17 Kathryn Tidrick, *Gandhi: A Political and Spiritual Life* (London: I.B. Tauris & Co. Ltd., 2008), p. 92.

18 Ajit K. Dasgupta, *Gandhi's Economic Thought* (New York: Routledge, 2003), p. 69.

19 Raghavan Iyer (ed.), *The Moral and Political Writings of Mahatma Gandhi: Volume I* (Oxford: Clarendon Press, 1986), p. 5.

20 Ghanshyam Shah, ed. *Re-reading Hind Swaraj: Modernity and subalterns* (London: Routledge, 2013).

21 Rudolph C. Heredia, "Interpreting Gandhi's Hind Swaraj", *Economic and Political Weekly 34*(24) (1999):1501.

22 Paul F. Power, "Gandhi in South Africa", *Journal of Modern African Studies* 7(3) (1969): 442.

23 Akeel Bilgrami, "Gandhi and Marx", *Social Scientist* 40(9/10) (2012): 5.

24 Lloyd I. Rudolph and Susanne Hoeber Rudolph, "Gandhi and the Debate about Civilisation", *Economic and Political Weekly* 50 (30) (2015):80.

25 Rajeshwar Pandey, *Gandhi and Modernisation* (New Delhi: Meenakshi Prakashan, 1979).

26 David Hardiman, *Gandhi in His Time and Ours: The Global Legacy of His Ideas* (Delhi: Permanent Black, 2003), p. 294.

27 Aditya Nigam, "Gandhi—the 'Angel of History': Reading 'Hind Swaraj' Today", *Economic and Political Weekly* 44(11) (2009):43.

28 Aditya Nigam, "Gandhi—the 'Angel of History': Reading 'Hind Swaraj' Today", p. 47.

29 Mahesh Gavaskar, "Gandhi's Hind Swaraj: Retrieving the Sacred in the Time of Modernity", *Economic and Political Weekly* 44(36) (2009): 14.

30 Dilip M. Menon, "An Eminent Victorian: Gandhi, *Hind Swaraj* and the Crisis of Liberal Democracy in the Nineteenth Century", *History of the Present* 7(1) (2017): 54.

31 Shaj Mohan and Divya Dwivedi, "Critical Nation", *Economic and Political Weekly* 42(48) (2007): 103.

32 Kumkum Sangari, "Who Is an Alien? Reading Gandhi", *Social Scientist*, 47(1–2 [548–549]: 27.

33 George Hendrick, "The Influence of Thoreau's 'Civil Disobedience' on Gandhi's Satyagraha", *New England Quarterly* 29(4) (1956): 470.

34 K. Raghavendra Rao, "The Political Theory in Hind Swaraj: A Preliminary Exploration", *Gandhi Marg*, 1(7) (1979): 471.

35 Partha Chatterjee, *Nationalist Thought and the Colonial World: A Derivative Discourse* (Minneapolis: University of Minnesota Press, 1986), p. 124.

36 Irfan Habib, "Mahatma Gandhi and the National Question", *Social Scientist* 47(1–2 [548–549]): 5.

37 Rajmohan Gandhi, *Mohandas: A True Story of a Man, His People and an Empire* (New Delhi: Penguin Books, 2006), p. 153.

38 Anthony J, Parel, ed. *Hind Swaraj and Other Writings* (Cambridge: Cambridge University Press, 1997).

39 Suresh Sharma and Tridip Suhrud, ed. *M.K. Gandhi's Hind Swaraj: A Critical Edition* (New Delhi: Orient BlackSwan, 2010).

40 S.R. Mehrotra, S.R., ed. *India Home Rule [Hind Swaraj]* (New Delhi: Promila & Co., Publishers in association with Bibliophile South Asia, 2010).

41 Usha Thakkar and Gita Dharmpal, ed. *Hind Swaraj: Mohandas Karamchand Gandhi* (Mumbai: Indus Source Book, 2019).

42 Mahadev Desai, ed. *M.K. Gandhi: Hind Swaraj or Indian Home Rule* (Ahmedabad: Navjivan Publishing House, 1939), p. iii.

43 Gopalkrishna Gandhi, "Foreword", In *An Autobiography or The Story of My Experiments with Truth: A Table of Concordance*, ed. Tridip Suhrud (New Delhi: Routledge, 2010), p. x.

44 Tridip Suhrud, "Hind Swaraj: Translating Sovereignty", In *Ten Books That Shaped the British Empire: Creating an Imperial Commons*, ed. Antoinette Burton and Isabel Hofmeyr (Durham: Duke University Press, 2014), p. 160.

Introduction

1 M.K. Gandhi, *Satyagraha in South Africa* (Madras: S. Ganesan, 1928), p. 509.

2 Ibid., p. 354.

3 Ibid., p. 354.

4 James D. Hunt, *Gandhi in London,* revised edition (New Delhi: Promila & Co., Publisher, 1993), pp. 55–156).

5   The Indian school of violence is an essential signpost for understanding Gandhi. The 26 January 1921 issues of *Young India* contained an article by Gandhi titled "Hind Swaraj" or "The Indian Home Rule". He uses the term "Indian school of violence" in it. He wrote that *Hind Swaraj* was written "during . . . [his] . . . return voyage from London to South Africa in answer to the Indian school of violence and its prototype in South Africa. I came in contact with every known Indian anarchist in London. Their bravery impressed me, but I felt that their zeal was misguided. I felt that violence was no remedy for India's ills and that her civilization required using a different and higher weapon for self-protection"(Gandhi, 1921, p. 27). This was added in the 1921 edition of *Hind Swaraj,* which made the book title *Hind Swaraj or The Indian Home Rule.* The article was retitled as *a word of explanation* in the revised new edition of 1939.

6   During his London visit in 1906, Gandhi met the founder of India House, Shyamji Krishnavarma (1857–1930). He was a barrister, a former reader at Oxford and the first Indian to receive an Oxford M.A. degree. In 1904, he established the Herbert Spencer Lectureship at Oxford while offering a fellowship to students. He also published the monthly journal *The Indian Sociologist,* which Herbert Spencer influenced. He was also the founder of the Indian Home Rule Society. Gandhi spent his first two nights during the London visit in 1906 at Indian House and later had extensive discussions with Krishnavarma on three Sunday evenings. Bhai Parmanand (an Arya Samaj missionary), J. C. Mukherji (who also wrote a weekly London Letter for *Indian Opinion*), and V.D. Savarkar (organizer of Free India Society and translator of the biography of Mazzini into Marathi) were present at India House at this time (Hunt, 1993, pp. 87–90). The 1978 edition of *Gandhi in London* by Hunt states that ". . . Savarkar and Gandhi would have a confrontation in 1909, but no evidence

remains of a 1906 meeting" (Hunt, 1978, p. 96). Rajmohan Gandhi states they met in 1906 (Gandhi, 2006, p. 150). In the substantive scholarship, the Indian School of Violence has identified with Krishnavarma and his group, which included Savarkar.

". . . Krishnavarma, in a sharp attack on *Hind Swaraj*, called Gandhi 'an admirer of Jesus Christ' who was trying to put into practice 'the extreme Christian Theory of suffering. Gandhi's identification of satyagraha with India, and of violence with the West, had clearly gone home, and Krishnavarma counter-attacked by linking Gandhi with a supposedly 'Western' religion . . . During Gandhi's lifetime satyagraha also marginalized . . . 'the Indian school of violence'"(Gandhi, 2006, p. 155). According to Bhikhu Parekh, Gandhi's *Hind Swaraj* "was both an answer to the Indian school of violence' and a 'severe condemnation of modern civilisation'" (Parekh, 1999, p. 172). Savarkar "received a scholarship to travel to Britain through the sponsorship of the former Dewan of Ratlam, Udaipur, and Junagadh, as well as the Oxford-educated Sanskritist Shyamji Krishnavarma. He was put up in Krishnavarma's residence, India House, in north London, with a group of Indian students who had also been sponsored to study in Britain"(Chaturvedi, 2022, pp. 47–48).

7   By 1909, Krishnavarma was taking shelter in Paris. Ganesh Savarkar was sentenced to life in the Andaman Islands. The murder of Curzon Wyllie disturbed Gandhi. On October 24, 1909, Gandhi spoke at a dinner at Nazam-ud-Din's restaurant. B.C. Pal chaired it (Hunt, 1993, p. 126). Virendranath Chattopadhyaya (1880–1942) was also present at the dinner. According to a police agent, "Dussera celebrations organised — to avoid Scotland Yard vigilance (inviting even the Englishmen): 24th October M.K. Gandhi of Transvaal presided in the dinner party and expressed disagreement with

Savarkar: so, he was criticized by Chatto and Savarkar"(Hunt, 1993, pp. 135–136).

Gandhi emphasized the significance of fasting during Navaratra (a nine-day fast). "Gandhi spoke of Sita, the pure, long-suffering one, while Savarkar spoke of Durga the violent and the slaying of Ravan, implying that nonviolence would be ineffectual without physical force"(Hunt, 1993, p. 127).

James Hunt states, "This was Gandhi's most public encounter with the radicals, and he spoke obliquely to them. It was a powerful moment for him, and he reflected on it in the weeks ahead. It would be re-lived in the writing of the dialogue in *Hind Swaraj*, on his homeward voyage"(Hunt, 1993, p. 127).

Vinayak Chaturvedi points out that "[b]y not specifically identifying Savarkar, or any other individual, *Hind Swaraj* may be considered Gandhi's response to emergent revolutionary thought, but there are passages that look like direct responses to Savarkar"(Chaturvedi, 2022, p. 84). *Joseph Mazzini* (1907) and *Hindu Pad-Padashahi* (1925) highlight differences with Gandhi directly. This is interesting to note "the primary Indian interpreters of Mazzini's writings were all present in London at the same time. In fact, Banerjea, Pal, and Savarkar were in a meeting together following the assassination of a colonial soldier-official, Curzon Wyllie, by an India House student, Madan Lal Dhingra, in July 1909. Gandhi, who had penned two essays on Mazzini, was also in London shortly after this point, as was Lajpat Rai, who provided the most comprehensive reception of Mazzini's life and work in India by writing a biography of Mazzini and translating his *The Duties of Man*"(Chaturvedi, 20022, p. 54). Besides drawing inspiration to form Abhinav Bharat Society from Mazzini's Young Italy formation, Savarkar ". . . was particularly interested in Mazzini's description of the strategies necessary for Italian independence: 'I am preparing a two-pronged plan to secure the help of Young Italy. Education and war training would support the war, and the war would support education"' (Chaturvedi, 2022, p. 67). Gandhi's *Joseph Mazzini* (1905) reads it as "a 'non-violent form of democratic nationalism'; this combined Mazzini's arguments about duty and self-rule with Gandhi's own conceptualisation of *swaraj* (self-rule)"(Chaturvedi, 2022, p. 52). Chapter two is *Hindavi Swaraj* of *Hindu Pad-Padashahi (1925)*. "Savarkar began his chapter called "Hindavi Swaraj"with a moment of violence: "The youth rose in rebellion."The contrast with Gandhi's non-violent interpretation of Hind Swaraj could hardly be more pointed"(Chaturvedi, 2022, p. 233).

8   M.K. Gandhi, *Satyagraha in South Africa* (Madras: S. Ganesan, 1928); M.K. Gandhi, *An Autobiography or the Story of My Experiments with Truth,* introduced with notes by Tridip Suhrud (Gurgaon: PRHI, 2018); James D. Hunt, *Gandhi in London,* revised edition (New Delhi: Promila & Co., Publisher, 1993); Ramchandra Guha, *Gandhi before India* (Random House, 2013); Rajmohan Gandhi, *Mohandas: A True Story of a Man, His People and an Empire* (New Delhi: Penguin, 2006); Anthony J . Parel, ed., *Hind Swaraj and Other Writings* (Cambridge: Cambridge University Press, 1997.

9   Regarding Liberalism and Empire, Uday Mehta makes an important observation: "The liberal association with the British Empire was extended and deep. Indeed, if one considers Locke's significant, even if only occasional, remarks on America and the constitution he wrote for the state of Carolina, the liberal involvement with the British Empire is broadly coeval with liberalism itself. 'With scarcely any exceptions, every British political thinker of note wrote on the empire and most of them wrote on the British Empire in India. More often than not, these writings were copious, as

in the cases of Edmund Burke, Jeremy Bentham, James Mill, Lord Macaulay, Sir Henry Maine, and John Stuart Mill; and when they were of a more occasional nature, as with Adam Smith, David Ricardo, and David Flume, they are nevertheless marked by a seriousness of purpose"(Mehta, 1999, p. 4).

10 James D. Hunt, *Gandhi in London,* revised edition (New Delhi: Promila & Co., Publisher, 1993), p. 38.

11 *Indian Opinion* Volumes 3–12 provide helpful information. *Gandhi Heritage Portal* (https://gandhiheritageportal.org/journals-by-gandhiji/indian-opinion) contains these volumes. These books are extremely helpful: M.K. Gandhi, *Satyagraha in South Africa* (Madras: S. Ganesan, 1928); D.G. Tendulkar, *Mahatma: Life of Mohandas Karamchand Gandhi,* volume one: 1869-1920 (New Delhi: Publication Division, Government of India, 1960); James D. Hunt, *Gandhi in London,* revised edition (New Delhi: Promila & Co., Publisher, 1993). *South African History Online: Towards a People's History* (SAHO) comprehensively details anti-Indian Legislation from the 1800s–1959 (https://www.sahistory.org.za/article/anti-indian-legislation-1800s-1959)._

12 M.K. Gandhi, *Satyagraha in South Africa* (Madras: S. Ganesan, 1928), p. 161.

13 Ibid., p. 163.

14 Ibid., p. 167.

15 Ibid., pp. 171–72.

16 Ibid., pp. 172–73.

17 Ibid., pp. 177–79.

18 *CWMG IX*, "Letter to Leo Tolstoy" (New Delhi: The Publications Division, Ministry of Information and Broadcasting, Government of India, 1963), pp. 445-46.

19 The friend was Pranjivandas Mehta. "At the insistence of and with the financial help given by P.J. Mehta, Gandhi got 20,000 copies of Tolstoy's '*Letter to a Hindoo*' printed and

distributed worldwide"(Mehrotra, 2010, p. 38). Gandhi said he ". . . wrote the entire Hind Swaraj for . . . [his] . . . friend Dr. Pranjivan Mehta. All the argument in the book is reproduced almost as it took place with him. . . . [He] stayed with Dr. Mehta for (more than) a month (at the Westminster Palace Hotel, 4 Victoria Street, London, S.W., in late 1909)"(*CWMG LXXI*, 1978, p. 238).

20 *CWMG IX,* "Letter to Leo Tolstoy" (New Delhi: The Publications Division, Ministry of Information and Broadcasting, Government of India, 1963), p. 446.

21 *CWMG XI,* "Tolstoy's Letter to Gandhiji" (New Delhi: The Publications Division, Ministry of Information and Broadcasting, Government of India, 1963), p. 593.

22 Anthony J . Parel, ed., *Hind Swaraj and Other Writings* (Cambridge: Cambridge University Press, 1997), p. xxix.

23 *CWMG IX,* "Letter to H.S.L. Polak" (New Delhi: The Publications Division, Ministry of Information and Broadcasting, Government of India, 1963), pp. 479–80.

24 S.R. Mehrotra, ed. *India Home Rule [Hind Swaraj]* (New Delhi: Promila& Co., Publishers in association with Bibliophile South Asia, 2010), p. 39.

25 D.G. Tendulkar, *Mahatma: Life of Mohandas Karamchand Gandhi, Volume One: 1869–1920* (New Delhi: Publication Division, Government of India, 1960), p. 105.

26 Suresh Sharma and Tridip Suhrud, ed. *M.K. Gandhi's Hind Swaraj: A Critical Edition* (New Delhi: Orient BlackSwan, 2010), p. xi.

27 Ibid.

28 Prabhudas Gandhi, *My Childhood with Gandhiji* (Ahmedabad: Navajivan Publishing House, 1957).

29 *Hind Swaraj* (Ahmedabad: Navjivan, 2009), pp. vi–vii.

30 *CWMG X,* Johannesburg (New Delhi: The Publications Division, Ministry of Information and Broadcasting, Government of India, 1963), p. 181.

31 *CWMG X,* Preface to "Indian Home Rule"(New Delhi: The Publications Division, Ministry of Information and Broadcasting, Government of India, 1963), pp.188–90.

32 *CWMG X,* Preface to "Indian Home Rule"(New Delhi: The Publications Division, Ministry of Information and Broadcasting, Government of India, 1963), pp. 188.

33 Hermann Kallenbach (1871–1945) is the name in Mahadev Desai's Preface to *Hind Swaraj,* 1938. This is also stated by footnote 2 of page 188 of *CWMG X.* He donated the land for the construction of Tolstoy Farm near the outskirts of Johannesburg in 1910, which became the central place for satyagraha.

34 "The History of the house", The Satyagraha House, https://www.satyagrahahouse.com/en/the-story-of-the-house.

35 *CWMG X,* "Letter to Tolstoy" (New Delhi: The Publications Division, Ministry of Information and Broadcasting, Government of India, 1963), p. 210.

36 *CWMG X,* Appendix III: "Tolstoy's Letter to Gandhiji" (New Delhi: The Publications Division, Ministry of Information and Broadcasting, Government of India, 1963), p. 505.

37 *CWMG X,* Preface to "Indian Home Rule"(New Delhi: The Publications Division, Ministry of Information and Broadcasting, Government of India, 1963), p. 188.

38 *CWMG X,* Appendix V: "W. J. Wybergh's Letter to Gandhiji"(New Delhi: The Publications Division, Ministry of Information and Broadcasting, Government of India, 1963), pp. 507–11.

39 Ibid., p. 508.

40 Ibid., p. 508.

41 Ibid., p. 508.

42 Ibid., p. 509.

43 Ibid., p. 509.

44 Ibid., p. 509.

45 Ibid., p. 510.

46 *CWMG X,* "Letter to W. J. Wybergh" (New Delhi: The Publications Division, Ministry of Information and Broadcasting, Government of India, 1963), pp. 246–50.

47 Ibid., p. 249.

48 Ibid., p. 249.

49 *CWMG X,* Our Publications (New Delhi: The Publications Division, Ministry of Information and Broadcasting, Government of India, 1963), p. 245.

50 Ibid.

51 Ibid.

52 *CWMG XV,* Statement on Laws for Civil Disobedience (New Delhi: The Publications Division, Ministry of Information and Broadcasting , Government of India, 1965), p. 192.

53 Ibid.

54 Ibid., p. 193.

55 *CWMG XXX,* "Letter to Labhshankar Mehta" (New Delhi: The Publications Division, Ministry of Information and Broadcasting, Government of India, 1968), p. 283.

56 *CWMG XXX,* Assorted Questions [-V] (New Delhi: The Publications Division, Ministry of Information and Broadcasting, Government of India, 1968), p. 325;

57 *CWMG XL,* Notes (New Delhi: The Publications Division, Ministry of Information and Broadcasting, Government of India, 1970), p. 202.

58 Ibid., p. 203.

59 *CWMG XIX,* Notes: On the Wrong Track (New Delhi: The Publications Division, Ministry of Information and Broadcasting, Government of India, 1966), p. 80.

60 Ibid., p. 81.

61 *CWMG XLII,* "Letter to Satish Chandra Das Gupta" (New Delhi: The Publications Division, Ministry of Information and Broadcasting, Government of India, 1970), p. 125.

62 Ibid.

63 *CWMG XLVI,* "Letter to K. Natarajan" (New Delhi: The Publications Division, Ministry of Information and Broadcasting, Government of India, 1971) p. 157.

64 Mahadev Desai, ed. *M.K. Gandhi: Hind Swaraj or Indian Home Rule* (Ahmedabad: Navjivan Publishing House, 1939), p. iv.

65 *The Aryan Path, IX* (9)(September 1938): 423.

66 Ibid.

67 *CWMG LXVII,* A Message to "The Aryan Path"(New Delhi: The Publications Division, Ministry of Information and Broadcasting , Government of India, 1976), p. 170 [fn1]

68 *CWMG LXXXVII,* "Speech at Prayer Meeting" (New Delhi: The Publications Division, Ministry of Information and Broadcasting , Government of India, 1983), p. 357.

69 Confidential. File no. 492 of 1910. 1911. Government, United Provinces. General Administration Department. January. A Proceedings –nos 21 of 36. Searching for and intercepting letters in the post containing seditious matter. Department: Home Political, Branch B, Identifier: PR_000003001329, File No.HOME   POLITICAL_B_1911_APR_76.   Location: Repository II. National Archive of India.

70 Ibid., p. 10.

71 Ibid., p. 10.

72 Ibid., p. 10.

73 Ibid., p. 10.

74 Ibid., pp. 10–11.

75 Ibid., p. 11.

76 Ibid.

77 Ibid.

78 Ibid.

79 Confidential. Home. 1910. Political. Part B. Proceedings May. Nos. 4/5. Seditious Books Found in the Possession of one Chibbu Parbhu who Recently Arrived in Bombay from

Durban. Identifier: PR_000003001187. File No. HOME
POLITICAL_B_1910_MAY_4-5. National Archive of India.
80 Ibid., p. 3; This was signed by H.C. Woodman, H.A. Stuart,
H.A. (damson).
81 Ibid., p. 5; noted in the Criminal Intelligence Office; Dy. No.
14660, from – The Madras S.B., No. M. 263., Dated March
18, 1910, Recd. March 24, 1910.
82 Ibid.
83 Ibid., p. 6.
84 Ibid., p. 9.
85 *Documentation* (1993). *Gandhi Marg 15* (2): 240.

In addition to the National Archive of India, I have also
referred to *Documentation* which was published in Gandhi
Marg: *Documentation* (1993). *Gandhi Marg, 15* (2), pp. 240–
54.

According to the editors of the Gandhi Marg concerning
*Report of the Gujarati Interpreter, High Court, Madras, March
15, 1910,* "*[t]his report has been made available to us by
Professor Anthony Parel who thanks Dr. R.J. Bingle of Oriental
and Indian Office Collections of the British Library for assisting
him to find the document, IOR: L/P/&J/6/1003, document J
and P 1468, of 1910 "Orders of forfeiture issue by maritime
local governments against Mr. Gandhi's "Hind Swaraj."Copies
of Crown-copyright records in the Oriental and India Office
Collections of the British Library appear by permission of the
Controller of Her Majesty's Stationery Office*"(Documentation,
1993, p. 241, original emphasis).
86 Confidential. Home. 1910. Political. Part B. Proceedings
May. Nos. 4/5. Seditious Books Found in the Possession of
one Chibba Parbhu who Recently Arrived in Bombay from
Durban. Identifier: PR_000003001187. File No. HOME
POLITICAL_B_1910_MAY_4-5. National Archive of
India. p. 8

87   Ibid., p. 10.
88   Ibid., pp. 10–31.
89   Confidential. File no. 492 of 1910. 1911. Government, United Provinces. General Administration Department. January. A Proceedings –nos 21 of 36. Searching for and intercepting letters in the post containing seditious matter. Department: Home Political, Branch B, Identifier: PR_000003001329, File No. HOME POLITICAL_B_1911_APR_76. Location: Repository II, pp. 9–14. National Archive of India.
90   Ibid., p. 10.
91   Ibid., p. 11.
92   Ibid., p. 12.
93   Ibid., p. 12.
94   Ibid., p. 14.
95   Ibid., p. 15.
96   Ibid., p. 16.
97   Secret. Simla Records.2.1910. Government of India. Home Department, Political-A. Proceedings, August 1910. Nos. 96-103. Interception under Section 26 of the India Post Office Act, 1898 (VI of 1898), prohibition of the entry into India under section 19 of the Sea Customs Act, 1878 (VIII of 1878), of a booklet entitled "Indian Home Rule"by M.K. Gandhi. National Archive of India.
98   Ibid., p. 8; Pro. No. 96.
99   Ibid., p. 8; Pro. No. 96.
100 Secret Simla Records. 2.1910. Government of India. Home Department, Political-A. Proceedings, August 1910. Nos. 96-103. Interception under Section 26 of the India Post Office Act, 1898 (VI of 1898), prohibition of the entry into India under section 19 of the Sea Customs Act, 1878 (VIII of 1878), of a booklet entitled "Indian Home Rule"by M.K. Gandhi. National Archive of India, p. 2.
101 Ibid., p. 2; Pro no. 6.

102 Ibid., p. 9; Pro no. 98.

103 Ibid., p. 9; Pro. 99.

104 Ibid., p. 9; Pro. 100.

105 Ibid., p. 9; Pro. 101.

106 Ibid., p.9.

107 Ibid., p. 10; Pro. no. 102.

108 Ibid., p. 10; Pro. no. 103.

109 Secret.1913 Government of India, Home Department, Political A. Proceedings May 1913, nos 9-13. 'Proposed action to be taken to strengthen the hands of the executive in dealing with sedition. The Press in India. Department: Home Political, Branch A, Identifier: PR_000003003442, File No. HOME_POLITICAL_A_1913_MAY_9-13, Location, Repository II, National Archive of India.

110 Ibid., p. 30.

111 Ibid., p. 30.

112 Ibid., p. 35.

113 Ibid., p. 51.

114 Ibid., p. 50.

115 M.K. Gandhi, *Indian Home Rule* (Phoenix: International Printing Press, 1910), pp. 3–6.

116 Ibid., pp. 7–8.

117 C. Rajagopalachari, "Note" in *M. K. Gandhi: Indian Home Rule* (Madras: Ganesh & Co, 1919).

118 M.K. Gandhi, *Indian Home Rule* (Madras: Ganesh & Co., 1919).

119 Sumit Sarkar, *Modern India (1885-1947)* (Delhi: Pearson, 2014), pp. 168–76.

120 M.K. Gandhi, "Swaraj in One Year", *Young India* II (38) (1920, September 22): 2.

121 Ibid., p. 1.

122 Ibid., p. 1.

123 Ibid., p.1.

124 Ibid., p. 2.
125 Ibid., p. 2.
126 M.K. Gandhi, "Swaraj in Nine Months", *Young India* 2(52)(1920): 6.
127 Ibid., p. 7.
128 M.K. Gandhi, "The Secret of My Swaraj", *Young India* 3(3) (1921): 20–21.
129 M.K. Gandhi, "Hind Swaraj or the Indian Home Rule", *Young India* 3 (4) *(1921, January 26):* 27.
130 Ibid.
131 Ibid.
132 Ibid.
133 Dhananjay Rai, *Poorna Swaraj: Constructive Programme: Its Meaning and Place by M.K. Gandhi* (Gurgaon: PRHI, 2023), pp. LXX-LXXII.
134 Ibid.
135 Dhananiay Keer, *Mahatma Gandhi: Political Saint and Unarmed Prophet* (Bombay: Popular Prakashan, 1973), pp.174–75.
136 M.K. Gandhi, "The Conditions of Swaraj", *Young India* 3(8) (1921): 59
137 M.K. Gandhi, "The Simla Visit", *Young India* 3 (21) (1921): 164.
138 M.K. Gandhi, "The Fear of Death", *Young India* 3(41) 1921: 326
139 M.K. Gandhi, "Independence", *Young India* 4(1) *(1922)*:4
140 M.K. Gandhi, "Swaraj or Death", *Young India* 7(35) (1925): 297.
141 M.K. Gandhi, "On the verge of It", *Young India* 7 (21) (1925):178.
142 M.K. Gandhi, "Theft on Railways", *Young India* 3(30) (1921): 238.

143   M.K. Gandhi, "Swaraj or Death", *Young India* 7 (35) (1925): 297.

144   M.K. Gandhi, "Sacrifice", *Young India* 8 (25) (1926): 226.

145   M.K. Gandhi, "Untouchability and Swaraj", *Young India* 6 (24) (1924):195.

146   M.K. Gandhi, "Interrogatories Answered", *Young India* 7 (5) 1925: 41.

147   M. K. Gandhi, "Teachers' Condition", *Young India* 7 (32) (1925): 276).

148   M.K. Gandhi, Mahadev Desai and His Successor', *Young India* 12 (8) (1930): 149

149   M.K. Gandhi, "Poor Man's *Swaraj*", *Young India* 13(13) (1931): 46-47.

150   M.K. Gandhi, "Question of Safeguards", *Young India* 13 (16) (1931): 78.

151   M.K. Gandhi, "Schoolmasters and Lawyers", *Young India* 6 (16) (1924): 130.

152   M.K. Gandhi, "Gandhiji's Speech at the A.I.C.C.", *Harijan* 8(33) (1940): 306

153   M.K. Gandhi, "Gandhiji's Press Statement", *Harijan* 10 (4) (1946): 31.

154   M.K. Gandhi, *Indian Home Rule*, second improved edition (Madras: S. Ganesan), pp. vii–xv.

155   Mahadev Desai, ed. *M.K. Gandhi: Hind Swaraj or Indian Home Rule* (Ahmedabad: Navjivan Publishing House, 1939), p. xii.

156   Ibid., pp. xxi–xv.

157   Mahadev Desai, ed. *M.K. Gandhi: Hind Swaraj or Indian Home Rule* (Ahmedabad: Navjivan Publishing House, 1938), p. vi, xxiv.

158   *The Holy Bible* (London: Hodder & Stoughton, 1996), p. 1061.

159   Leo Tolstoy, *The Kingdom of God is Within You*, introduction by Kenneth Rexroth (New York: The Noonday Press, 1970), p. 47.

160   Ibid., p. 19.

161   Ibid.

162   *CWMG IX*, "Letter to Manilal Gandhi" (New Delhi: The Publications Division, Ministry of Information and Broadcasting, Government of India, 1963), p. 205.

163   *CWMG XXX VII*, "Speech on Birth Centenary of Tolstoy" (pp. 260–68) (New Delhi: The Publications Division, Ministry of Information and Broadcasting , Government of India, 1970), p. 261.

164   Ibid., p. 262.

165   Ibid., p. 263.

166   Ibid., p. 265.

167   Ibid.

168   *CWMG XXX VII,* "Speech on Birth Centenary of Tolstoy" (pp. 260–68) (New Delhi: The Publications Division, Ministry of Information and Broadcasting, Government of India, 1970), p. 261, 266.

169   Ibid., p. 267.

170   Ibid., p. 268.

171   (Parel, 1997, p. xxxvii).

172   (Gandhi, 2018, p. 179).

173   M.K. Gandhi, *An Autobiography or the Story of My Experiments with Truth,* introduced with notes by Tridip Suhrud (Gurgaon: PRHI, 2018), p. 243.

174   Leo Tolstoy, *What is Art?* trans. and introduction by Aylmer Maude (New York: Funk & Wagnalls Company), p. 50.

175   Ibid., p. 47.

176   Ibid., p. 50.

177   Ibid.

178   Ibid., pp. 198–99.

179   *CWMG XXXV*, "Letter to Maninlal and Sushila Gandhi" (New Delhi: The Publications Division, Ministry of Information and Broadcasting, Government of India, 1969), p. 363.

180   Ibid.

181   Leo Tolstoy, *The Slavery of Our Times*, translation and introduction by Aylmer Maude (Maldon Essex: The Free Agre Press), p. 92.

182   Ibid., p. 101.

183   Ibid.

184   Ibid., p. 102.

185   Ibid.

186   Ibid., pp. 120–21.

187   Ibid., p. 124.

188   Ibid., p. 75.

189   Ibid., p. 87.

190   Ibid., pp. 79–80.

191   Leo Tolstoy. *The First Step: An Essay on Morals of Diets*, translation by Aylmer Maude and introduction by William E.E. Axon (Manchester: Albert Braodbent, 1900), p. 21.

192   Ibid., p. 22.

193   Ibid., p. 33.

194   Ibid., p. 33.

195   Ibid., p. 3.

196   Ibid., p. 34.

197   Ibid., p. 35.

198   Ibid., p. 37.

199   Ibid., p. 38.

200   Ibid., p. 39.

201   Ibid.

202   Ibid.

203   Ibid., p. 41.

204   Ibid., p. 42.

205 Ibid., p. 43.

206 Ibid., p. 60.

207 Ibid.

208 Leo Tolstoy, "How shall we Escape?" in *What is Religion? And Other New Articles and Letters,* trans. V. Tchertkoff and A. C. Fifield (New York: Thomas Y. Crowell & Company Publishers, 1902), p. 123.

209 Ibid., p. 124.

210 Ibid., p. 4.

211 Ibid., pp. 122–33.

212 *CWMG X,* "Preface to Tolstoy's *Letter to a Hindoo*"(New Delhi: The Publications Division, Ministry of Information and Broadcasting , Government of India, 1963), pp. 1–5.

213 *CWMG X,* "Letter to Tolstoy" (New Delhi: The Publications Division, Ministry of Information and Broadcasting, Government of India, 1963), p. 210.

214 *CWMG X,* "Preface to Tolstoy's *Letter to a Hindoo*"(New Delhi: The Publications Division, Ministry of Information and Broadcasting, Government of India, 1963), p. 1.

215 Ibid., p. 1.

216 Ibid., p. 2.

217 Ibid.,

218 Ibid.

219 Ibid., p. 3.

220 Ibid.

221 Ibid., p. 4.

222 Ibid.

223 Ibid.

224 Ibid., pp. 4–5.

225 Ibid.,p. 5.

226 Robert Harborough Sherard, *The White Slaves of England* (London: James Bowden, 1897), p. 32.

227 Ibid., p. 41.

NOTES 136

228   Ibid., pp. 41–42.
229   Ibid., p. 66.
230   Ibid., pp. 73–74.
231   Ibid., p. 83.
232   Ibid., p. 118.
233   Ibid., p. 135.
234   Ibid., pp. 137–38.
235   Ibid., p. 157.
236   Ibid., p. 165.
237   Ibid., p. 181.
238   Ibid., p. 198.
239   Ibid., p. 219.
240   Ibid., p. 233.
241   Ibid., p. 239.
242   Edward Carpenter, *Civilisation: Its Cause and Cure* (London: Swan Sonnenschein & Co., 1889), p. 1.
243   Ibid., p. 2.
244   Ibid., pp. 2–3.
245   Ibid., p. 3.
246   Ibid., p. 5.
247   Ibid., pp. 8–13.
248   Ibid., 15–21.
249   Ibid., p. 22.
250   Ibid., pp. 23–49.
251   Ibid., p. 49.
252   Ibid., pp. 52–85.
253   Ibid., p. 85.
254   Ibid., p. 96.
255   Ibid., p. 97.
256   Ibid., p. 106.
257   Ibid., p.107.
258   Ibid., p. 108.
259   Ibid., p.124.

260   Ibid., p. 128.
261   Thomas F. Taylor, *The Fallacy of Speed* (London: A.C. Fifield), p. 9.
262   Ibid., pp. 21–22.
263   Ibid., p. 24.
264   Ibid., p. 25.
265   Ibid., pp. 26–27.
266   Ibid., p. 29.
267   Ibid., p. 30.
268   Ibid., pp. 35–47.
269   Ibid., pp. 51–63.
270   Ibid., p. 63.
271   Ibid., p. 63.
272   "Jhadap ane tena matha parinmo", *Indian Opinion* 8 (49): 793.
273   Godfrey Blount, *A New Crusade: An Appeal* (London, The Simple Life Press, 1903), p. iii.
274   Ibid., pp. iv–vi.
275   Ibid., pp. vi–vii.
276   Ibid., pp. vii–xv.
277   Elizabeth P. Peabody, *Aesthetic Papers* (Boston: The Editor, 13, West Street, 1849), p. iii.
278   Henry David Thoreau, *On the Duty of Civil Disobedience* (London: The Simple Life Press, 1903), p. 7.
279   Ibid., p. 7.
280   Ibid., p. 7.
281   Ibid., p. 9.
282   Ibid.
283   Ibid.
284   Ibid., pp. 10–11.
285   William Paley, *The Principles of Moral and Political Philosophy* (Boston: Richardson and Lord), p. 309; Henry

David Thoreau, *On the Duty of Civil Disobedience* (London: The Simple Life Press, 1903), pp. 12–13.

286 Ibid., p. 14.

287 Ibid., p. 18.

288 Henry David Thoreau, *Life Without Principle* (London: The Simple Life Press, 1905), p. 6.

289 Ibid., pp. 11–21.

290 Ibid., p. 26.

291 Ibid., p. 26.

292 Ibid., p. 31.

293 John Ruskin, *Unto This Last,* ed. Susan Cunnington (London: M. Dent & Sons Ltd, 1920), p. 15.

294 Ibid., pp. 15–16.

295 Ibid., p. 45.

296 Ibid.

297 Ibid., pp. 45–46.

298 Ibid., p. 48.

299 Ibid., p. 57.

300 Ibid., p. 58.

301 Ibid., p. 67.

302 Ibid., p. 92.

303 Ibid., p. 116.

304 Ibid., p. 119.

305 Ibid., p. 127.

306 M.K. Gandhi, *An Autobiography or the Story of My Experiments with Truth,* introduced with notes by Tridip Suhrud (Gurgaon: PRHI, 2018), pp. 470–71.

307 Ibid., p. 471.

308 John Keats, *Endymion A Poetic Romance* (London: Taylor and Hesse, 1818), p. 3.

309 John Ruskin, *A Joy Forever the Two Paths* (London: George Allen & Sons, Ruskin House, 1911), p. 9.

310 Ibid., pp. 20–22.

311 Ibid., p. 53.

312 Ibid., p. 56.
313 Ibid., p. 93.
314 Ibid., p. 99.
315 Ibid., p. 112.
316 Ibid., p. 121.
317 Giuseppe Mazzini, *The Duties of Man* (London: Chapman & Hall, 193, Piccadilly, 1862), p. ix–xii.
318 Ibid., pp.15-19.
319 Ibid., p. 19.
320 Ibid., p. 19.
321 Ibid., p. 20.
322 Ibid., p. 22.
323 Ibid.
324 Ibid., p. 23.
325 Ibid., p. 27.
326 Ibid., pp. 28–66.
327 Ibid., p. 82.
328 Ibid., p. 91.
329 Ibid., p. 91.
330 Ibid., p. 93.
331 Ibid.
332 Ibid., p. 94.
333 Ibid.
334 Ibid., pp. 96–98.
335 Ibid., p. 99.
336 Ibid., pp. 100–01.
337 Ibid., p. 102.
338 Ibid., p. 121.
339 Ibid., pp. 130–31.
340 Ibid., p. 132.
341 Ibid., p. 133.
342 Ibid., p. 134.
343 Ibid., p. 141.

344   Ibid., p. 152.

345   Ibid., p. 162.

346   Ibid., pp. 217–20.

347   Plato, *Euthyphro, Apology, Crito, Phaedo, Phaedrus*, introduction by W.R. Lamb and trans. Harold North Fowler (Cambridge, Mass.: Harvard University Press, 1914).

348   Phiroze Vasunia, "Gandhi and Socrates", *African Studies* 74 (2) (2015): 179.

349   W.R.M. Lamb, "Introduction to the Apology", in *Plato*: *Euthyphro, Apology, Crito, Phaedo, Phaedrus*, trans. Harold North Fowler (Cambridge, Mass.: Harvard University Press, 1914), pp. 63–67.

350   Plato, *Euthyphro, Apology, Crito, Phaedo, Phaedrus*, introduction by W.R.M Lamb and trans. Harold North Fowler (Cambridge, Mass.: Harvard University Press. 1914), p. 69.

351   Ibid., p. 83.

352   Ibid., pp. 111–13.

353   Ibid., p. 113.

354   *CWMG VIII,*   Story of a Soldier of Truth-I (Preface) (New Delhi: The Publications Division, Ministry of Information and Broadcasting, Government of India, 1962), pp. 172–74.

355   *CWMG VIII,* Story of a Soldier of Truth-II (New Delhi: The Publications Division, Ministry of Information and Broadcasting, Government of India, 1962), pp. 185–87.

356   *CWMG VIII,* Story of a Soldier of Truth-III (New Delhi: The Publications Division, Ministry of Information and Broadcasting, Government of India, 1962), pp. 196–99.

357   *CWMG VIII,* Story of a Soldier of Truth-IV (New Delhi: The Publications Division, Ministry of Information and Broadcasting, Government of India, 1962), pp. 212–14.

358 *CWMG VIII,* Story of a Soldier of Truth (New Delhi: The Publications Division, Ministry of Information and Broadcasting, Government of India, 1962), pp. 217–21.

359 *CWMG VIII,* Story of a Soldier of Truth (New Delhi: The Publications Division, Ministry of Information and Broadcasting, Government of India, 1962), pp. 227–29.

360 Max Nordau, *Conventional Lies of Our Civilization* (Chicago: Laird & Lee, Publishers, 1884).

361 Ibid., p. 3.

362 Ibid., p. 4.

363 Ibid., p.12.

364 Ibid., p. 17.

365 Ibid., p. 24.

366 Ibid., p. 27.

367 Ibid., p. 28.

368 Ibid., p. 30.

369 Ibid., pp. 35–36.

370 Ibid., p. 40.

371 Ibid., p. 47.

372 Ibid., p. 60.

373 Ibid., p. 63.

374 Ibid., p. 69.

375 Ibid., p. 71.

376 Ibid., p. 72.

377 Ibid.

378 Ibid., pp. 72–73.

379 Ibid., p. 78.

380 Ibid., p. 81.

381 Ibid., p. 82.

382 Ibid., pp. 84–85.

383 Ibid., p. 94.

384 Ibid., p. 101.

385 Ibid., p. 126.

386 Ibid., pp.129–138.
387 Ibid., p. 158.
388 Ibid., pp. 162–172.
389 Ibid., p. 172.
390 Ibid., p. 174.
391 Ibid., p. 186.
392 Ibid., p. 188.
393 Ibid., p. 190.
394 Ibid., p. 192.
395 Ibid., p. 197.
396 Ibid., p. 198.
397 Ibid., pp. 200–03.
398 Ibid., p. 204.
399 Ibid., p. 217.
400 Ibid., p. 220.
401 Ibid., p. 231.
402 Ibid., p. 233.
403 Ibid., p. 249.
404 Ibid., p. 260.
405 Ibid., p. 274.
406 Ibid., p. 283.
407 Ibid., p. 290.
408 Ibid., pp. 319–22.
409 Max Nordau, *Paradoxes* (Chicago: L Schick, Publisher, 1886), p. 3.
410 Ibid., p. 40.
411 Ibid.
412 Dadabhai Naoroji, *The Poverty of India: Papers and Statistics* (London: Winckworth Foulger & Co, The Aldine Press) p. 1.
413 Ibid., p. 79.
414 Ibid., p. 109.
415 Ibid., pp. 162–163.

416   Ibid., p. 178.

417   Dadabhai Naoroji (1901), *Poverty and Un-British rule in India* (London: Swan Sonnenschein & Co., LIM, Paternoster Square), p. v.

418   Ibid., pp. vi–vii.

419   Dadabhai Naoroji, *The Poverty of India: Papers and Statistics* (London: Winckworth Foulger & Co, The Aldine Press), pp. viii–x.

420   Romesh Chunder Dutt, *The Economic History of India, Volume I* (New Delhi: Publications Division, Ministry of Information and Broadcasting, Government of India), p. xxi.

421   Ibid., pp. xxii–xxv.

422   Ibid., p. xxv.

423   Ibid., pp. xxvi–xxvii.

424   Ibid., pp. xxviii.

425   Ibid., p. xxx.

426   Ibid., p. 286.

427   Dutt, 2006a, p. 286).

428   (Dutt, 2006b, page number not mentioned).

429   Romesh Chunder Dutt, *The Economic History of India, Volume II* (New Delhi: Publications Division, Ministry of Information and Broadcasting, Government of India).

430   Ibid.

431   Ibid., p. 380.

432   Ibid., p. 380.

433   Ibid., p. 380.

434   Ibid., p. 383.

435   Ibid., p. 386.

436   Henry Sumner Maine, *Village-communities in the East and West* (New York: Henry Hold and Company, 1889), p. 18.

437   Ibid., p. 20.

438   Ibid., p. 57.

439   Ibid., p. 57.
440   Ibid., p. 60.
441   Ibid., p. 67.
442   Ibid., p. 103.
443   Ibid., p. 117.
444   Ibid., p. 123.
445   Ibid., p. 125.
446   Ibid., p. 175.
447   Anuradha Veeravalli highlights swaraj and sovereignty in Gandhi's discourse (Veeravalli, 2011, pp. 65–69). Gandhi's Swaraj offers an alternative to civil society and state relationship relations and goes beyond the axioms of modern sovereignty, i.e. supreme authority. i.e., superior authority and territory. The three differences are:

> (1) it presupposed the necessary differentiation and separation of civil society from the state, in their origin and constitution. (2) The possibility of self reform, rather than control over, or freedom from the other was seen as a necessary condition of sovereignty. (3) It disposed of territory as a definitional condition of sovereignty; rather sovereignty defined the relation/frontier (not boundaries) between territories of different nations, and of self and other (Veeravalli, 2011, p. 67).

Swaraj is not distancing from others or establishing jurisdiction over territories. "It signifies a frontier of mutual respect, love/non-violence and service of the neighbour/ opponent located in the material and political culture of the people rather than in a relation of power, mutual fear, and exploitation"(Veeravalli, 2011, p. 68). Accordingly, *sovereignty* is defined as dialectic between self and others and a condition of possible dialogue, not

,territoriality. "Sovereignty is not power over another but being witness to the dialectic of self and other; a frontier is not a boundary between territories but a point of their meeting, and a condition for possible dialogue"(Veeravalli, 2011, p. 69). Ajay Skaria provides a critical analysis of sovereignty. "Relinquishing sovereignty, satyagrahis must strive for an equality of and with the minor. As that phrase suggests, the minor is never simply an individual—minority names here rather the community that perdures without sovereignty, and yet without submitting to majority or sovereignty"(Skaria, 2016, p. 9). The core of "Gandhi's equality of the minor is what could be called surrender without subordination"(Skaria, 2016, p. 9). For Aishwarya Kumar, "Like *Annihilation of Caste, Hind Swaraj* is written as a moral treatise on responsibility, partly as political essay in sovereignty"(Kumar, 2015, p. 11).

448   "The existence of a law is one thing: its *merits* or *demerits* are another thing. Whether a law *be*, is one inquiry: whether it *ought* to be, or whether it agree with a given or assumed test, is another and a distinct inquiry"(Austin, 1861, p. 233).

449   John Austin, *The Province of Jurisprudence Determined: The First Part of A Series Of Lectures on Jurisprudence, Or the Philosophy of Positive Law* (London: John Edward Taylor, Little Queen Street, Lincoln's Inn Fields, 1861).

450   Ibid., p. xli.

451   Ibid., p. 48.

452   Ibid., p. 169.

453   H.L.A. Hart, *The Concept of Law* (Oxford: Oxford University Press, 1961), pp. 78–79.

454   Ronald Dworkin, *Justice for Hedgehogs* (Cambridge, Mass.: The Belknap Press of Harvard University Press, 2011), p. 414.

455   Joseph Raz, *The Authority of Law Essays on Law and Morality* (Oxford: Oxford University Press, 2009), p. 272.

456   John Rawls, *A Theory of Justice* (Cambridge, Mass.: The Belknap Press of Harvard University Press, 1999), p. 329.

457   Ibid., p. 330.

458   Ronald Dworkin, *Justice for Hedgehogs* (Cambridge, Mass.: The Belknap Press of Harvard University Press), p. 265.

459   Akeel Bilgrami, "Gandhi, the Philosopher", *Economic and Political Weekly* 38(39)(2003): p. 4162.

460   Karuna Mantena, "Another Realism: The Politics of Gandhian Nonviolence", *American Political Science Review* 106 (2) (2012), p. 455.

461   (Kher, 1996, p. v)

462   Charles DiSalvo, *The Man before the Mahatma: M.K. Gandhi, Attorney at Law* (Noida: Random House, 2012), pp. xi–xiii.

463   Ibid.

464   Ramin Jahanbegloo, *The Disobedient Indian: Towards a Gandhian Philosophy of Dissent* (New Delhi: Speaking Tiger, 2018).

465   Carl Schmitt, *The Concept of the Political* (Chicago: The University of Chicago Press, 2007).

466   Chantal Mouffe, "Deliberative Democracy or Agonistic Pluralism?", *Social Research* 66(3) (1999): 745–58; Chantal Mouffe, *Agonistics. Thinking the World Politically* (London: Verso, 2013).

467   Chantal Mouffe, "Deliberative Democracy or Agonistic Pluralism?", *Social Research* 66(3) (1999): 754.

468   Ibid., pp. 755–56

469   *CWMG XLIII,* Duty of Disloyalty (New Delhi: The Publications Division, Ministry of Information and Broadcasting, Government of India, 1971), p. 133.

470   M.K. Gandhi, *Young India: 1919-1922* (Madras: S. Ganesan, 1924), p. 21.

471   Ibid., p. 941.

472   Ibid., p. 944.

473   M.K. Gandhi, *Sarvodaya: The Welfare of All* (Ahmedabad: Navajivan Publishing House, 1954), p. 3.

474   M.K. Gandhi, *Indian Home Rule* (Phoenix: International Printing Press, 1910), p. 77.

475   Ibid., p. 80

476   Political (Special) Department file no. 1571 of 1917 (Misra, 1963, pp. 69–70).

477   M.K. Gandhi, *An Autobiography or the Story of My Experiments with Truth,* introduced with notes by Tridip Suhrud (Gurgaon: PRHI, 2018), p. 638; B.B. Misra, *Select Documents on Mahatma Gandhi's Movement in Champaran 1917-1* (Patna: The Government of Bihar, 1963), pp. 69–70.

478   M.K. Gandhi , "Tempering with Loyalty", *Young India* 3 (39) (29 September 1921), p. 309.

479   M.K. Gandhi, "A Puzzle and a Solution", *Young India* 3 (50) (15 December 1921), p. 418.

480   M.K. Gandhi, "Shaking the Manes", *Young India* 4 (8) (23 February 1922), p. 119.

481   M.K. Gandhi, *Young India: 1919–1922* (Madras: S. Ganesan, 1924), p. 1054.

482   Ibid., Ibid.,p. 1053.

483   Thomas Hill Green, *Lectures on the Principles of Political Obligation and Other Writings,* ed. Paul Harris and John Morrow (Cambridge: Cambridge University Press, 1986).

484   Carole Pateman, *The Problem of Political Obligation: A Critique of Liberal Theory* (Berkeley: University of California Press, 1985).

485   Ibid., p. 178.

486   Robert Paul Wolff, *In Defense of Anarchism* (New York: Harper and Row, 1970).

487   Richard Dagger, *Rights, Citizenship, and Republican Liberalism: Civic Virtues* (Oxford: Oxford University Press, 1997), p. 79.

488   1. Communal Unity 2. Removal of Untouchability 3. Prohibition 4. Khadi 5. Other Village Industries 6. Village Sanitation 7. New or Basic Education 8. Adult Education 9. Women 10. Education in Health and Hygiene 11. Provincial Language 12. National Language 13. Economic Equality 14. Kisans 15. Labour 16. Adivasis 17. Lepers 18. Students. For more on the constructive programme, kindly refer to Rai (2023).

489   This section's comprehensive versions are part of my forthcoming edited volume *Debating Swaraj*, in which my introduction and chapter on *Hind Swaraj: Metaphors of Political Community* reflect this debate.

HIND SWARAJ/INDIAN HOME RULE

Preface to the English translation

1   The public is a modern arrival for horizontal space and egalitarian inclusiveness. For Gandhi, public means the publicness of the issues that defy the distinction between private and public (*CWMG LXXXVIII*, 1983, p. 123–26). In this, public opinion becomes very crucial. According to him, he had "...one great thing with ...[him]... that is public opinion. Public opinion has tremendous power...Tolstoy...has said that the greatest power on earth is public opinion"(*CWMG LXXXVIII*, 1983, p. 124).

2   Hermann Kallenbach (1871–1945): An important ally and collaborator of Gandhi in South Africa and a principal architect of Tolstoy Farm (1910), which was established near Johannesburg on his land, which was around 1100 acres. Gandhi said, "When we thought of accommodating the families of satyagrahi prisoners in Johannesburg in one

place, Kallenbach lent the use of his big farm without any rent"(Gandhi, 1928, p. 274). Mahadev Desai mentions his name in both 1938/1939 editions of the *Hind Swaraj.* "Gandhiji had translated the book for Mr Kallenbach"(Desai, 1939, p. xxii).

3   M.K. Gandhi, હિંદ સ્વરાજ્ય, *Indian Opinion* 7(50) (11 December 1909; chapter 1–12): 784–96; M.K. Gandhi, હિંદ સ્વરાજ્ય, *Indian Opinion* 7(51) (18 December 1909; chapter 13–20): 800–12.

4   Isabel Hofmeyr offers a fascinating account of Gandhi's Printing Press which was "experiments in slow reading". According to Hofmeyr, "[o]pening its doors in Durban in 1898, the International Printing Press (IPP) (of which Gandhi was a sometime proprietor) consisted of a small jobbing operation that from 1903 began printing *Indian Opinion.* A year and a half after the launch of the paper, the IPP moved to Phoenix, Gandhi's first ashram, fourteen miles north of the city. From here, the IPP continued to produce *Indian Opinion,* and both the press and the paper found themselves protagonists in the larger story of satyagraha, or passive resistance, in South Africa, which unfolded between 1906 and 1914"(Hofmeyr, 2013, pp. 2–3). Between 1903 and 1914, thirty pamphlets were published by the International Printing Press (Hofmeyr, 2013, p.98). Some of the "pamphlets reprinted from *Indian Opinion*" in English were: "J. L. P. Erasmus. *The Story of the Ramayana.* Phoenix: International Printing Press, 1905; *For Passive Resisters.* Phoenix: International Printing Press, 1907; M. S. Maurice. *Ethics of Passive Resistance.* Phoenix: International Printing Press, 1907; [H. S. L. Polak]. *A Book and Its Misnomer.* Phoenix: International Printing Press, 1907; M. K. Gandhi. *Indian Home Rule.* Phoenix: International Printing Press, 1910; Leo Tolstoy. *Letter to a Hindoo.* Phoenix: International Printing Press, 1910 (Hofmeyr, 2013, p. 165). *Indian Home Rule* and *Letter to a Hindoo* mentioned "No

Rights Reserved", which was a way of functioning beyond the control of the market and the state (Hofmeyr, 2013, p. 67).

5 Started in 1903.

6 Leo Tolstoy (1828–1910): Gandhi refers to *The Kingdom of God is Within You*, *What is Art?*, *The Slavery of Our Times*, *The First Step*, *How Shall We Escape?* and *Letter to a Hindoo* as follow-up readings. Joseph Doke, in *M. K. Gandhi-An Indian Patriot in South Africa* (the first biography of Gandhi in 1909), refers to Gandhi as "a disciple of Tolstoy" (Doke, 1967, p. 8). Tolstoy Farm was established in 1910 for Satyagraha and Satyagrahis. Gandhi repeatedly refers to Tolstoy and Tolstoy Farm in *Satyagraha in South Africa* and *Autobiography*.

7 John Ruskin (1819–1900): Gandhi refers to his two books in *Hind Swaraj*. Gandhi develops his notion of *Sarvodaya* through Ruskin.

8 Henry David Thoreau (1817–1962): Gandhi refers to his work *On the Duty of Civil Disobedience*, which profoundly influenced him.

9 Ralph Waldo Emerson (1803–82): His essay on "self-reliance"is remarkable. For him, "[d]iscontent is the want of self-reliance". (Emerson, 1908, p. 46). Moreover, "the reliance on property, including the reliance on the government, which protects it, is the want of self-reliance"(Emerson, 1908, p. 56). "A political victory, a rise in rents, the recovery of your sick, the return of your absent friend, or some other quite external event raises your spirits, and you think good days are preparing for you. Do not believe it. It can never be so. Nothing can bring you peace but yourself. Nothing can bring you peace but the triumph of principle"(Emerson, 1908, p. 59).

10 Condemnation of the British imperialism and after-effect.

Foreword

1 Some chapters: 1909-GE: વીસ પ્રકરણ; 1959-HE: बीस अध्याय [twenty chapters].

2   Venture to place: 1909-GE: હિંમત કરું છું/*himmat karu chhu*/ dare to put.

3   Dialogue: 1909-GE: સંવાદ (*samvad*); 1959-HE: संवाद.

4   Reader: 1909-GE: વાચક (*vachak*); 1959-HE:पाठक.

5   Editor: 1909-GE: અધિપતિ(*adhipati*); 1959-HE: संपादक.

6   M.K. Gandhi: 1909-GE: મોહનદાસ કરમચંદ ગાંધી [Mohandas Karamchand Gandhi]; 1959-GE: मोहनदास करमचंद गाँधी.

Chapter 1: Indian Home Rule

1   Indian Home Rule: 1909-GE: હિન્દ સ્વરાજ્ય (*Hind Swarajya*); RNE: Hind Swaraj or Indian Home Rule; 1959-HE: हिंद स्वराज्य.

2   The Congress and its Officials: 1909-GE: કોંગ્રેસ અને તેના કારભારી (*Congress ane tena karabhari*);1959-HE: कांग्रेस और उसके कर्ता-धर्ता;કારભારી (*karabhari*) also means administrator.

     The Indian National Congress' first session took place in Bombay on 28–30 December 1885. W.C. Bonnerjee and A.O. Hume were elected president and general secretary (by implication), respectively. The total number of delegates was seventy-two. Promotion of personal intimacy and friendship, eradication of race, creed, or provincial prejudices; authoritative record of educated classes in India; and working of native politicians in the public interest were broad objectives (Zaidi and Zaidi, 1976, pp. 35–47). According to Briton Martin, Jr., "[a]t the beginning of 1885, the educated Indian leaders were still searching for their role and purpose in British Indian society. By the end of the year, they had found both. "New India" stood forth unveiled. It stood in opposition to official policy" (Martin, 1969, p. 311).

3   Home Rule wave: 1909-GE: સ્વરાજ્યનો પવન (*Swaarajyane pavana*); 1959-HE: स्वराज्य की हवा.

4   RNE: Indians seem to be eager to acquire rights. The sentence in Gujarati also denotes "the uphill" task of acquiring rights.

5   RNE: You have put the question well, but the answer is not easy.

6   RNE: One of the objects of a newspaper is to understand popular feeling and to give expression to it, another is to arouse among the people certain desirable sentiments, and the third is fearlessly to expose popular defects.

7   RNE: Professor Gokhale, in order to prepare the nation, embraced poverty and gave twenty years of his life.

8   Badruddin Tyabji (1844–1906): President of Indian National Congress (1887); Barrister; Member of the Bombay Legislative Council (1882); former judge (1895) and chief justice (1902) of the Bombay High Court. Gandhi writes in *Autobiography* about him: "Badruddin Tyabji's wonderful power of argument inspires the judges with awe" (Gandhi, 2018, p. 185).

9   Tree does not grow in one day: 1909-GE: ઉતાવળે આંબા ન પાકે (*Utavaḷe aamba na pake*); 1959-HE: उतावली से आम नहीं पकते,दाल नहीं चुरती (*Mangoes don" t ripen, and pulses do not cook due to haste.*)

10 RNE: The fact that you have checked me and that you do not want to hear about the well-wishers of India shows that, for you, at any rate, Home Rule is yet far away.

11 The father of nation: 1909-GE: હિંદના દાદા/*Hindna dada*; 1959-GE: हिन्द के दादा.

12 Dadabhai Naoroji (1825–1917) highlighted the high taxation and wealth being drained from India to England. He was elected as a member of Parliament in England in 1892. He presided over the annual sessions of the Indian National Congress in 1886, 1893 and 1906. He wrote *Poverty and Un-British Rule in India* (1901). Gandhi mentioned the book in *Hind Swaraj* for a follow-up study. According to Naoroji, the title of the book (*The Poverty And Un-British Rule In India*) shows that "the present system of government is destructive

and despotic to the Indians and un-British and suicidal to Britain" (Naoroji, 1901, p. v). Moreover, "[t]he existing system of British Rule is an un-British, debasing, destructive, despotic and impoverishing Rule" (Naoroji, 1901, p. 624).

13 RNE: It is a mark of wisdom not to kick away the very step from which we have risen higher.

14 Grand Old Man of India: 1909-GE: હિંદના દાદા (*Hindana dada*); 1959-HE: हिन्द के दादा.

15 We must admit that he is the author of Nationalism: 1909-GE:તેની પછાડી હીંદી પ્રજા છે એમ તો આપણે કહેવુંજ પડશે (*Teni pachadi Hindi praja chhe ema to Apane kahevunja padase*); RNE: We must admit that he is the author of nationalism; 1959-HE: उनके पीछे (सारी) हिन्दी जनता है, यह तो हमें कहना ही पड़ेगा."हिन्दीजनता" or Hindi people should be read as *Hindustani people or Indian people*.

16 RNE: should

17 Gopal Krishna Gokhale (1866–1915) was considered Gandhi's political guru. He was also the former president of the Indian National Congress (1905), the founder of the Servants of India Society (1905), and sympathetic to Indians in South Africa. Gokhale and Gandhi developed a very close relation towards each other. Therefore, according to Gandhi, Gokhale said this about *Hind Swaraj:* "I [Gandhi] may note in this connection that Gokhale used to laugh at some of my ideas in *Hind Swaraj* or *Indian Home Rule* and say: 'After you have stayed a year in India, your views will correct themselves'" (Gandhi, 2018, p. 591).

18 RNE: He has constituted himself a great friend of the English, he says that we have to learn a great deal from them, that we have to learn their political wisdom, before we can talk of Home Rule.

19 RNE: We believe that those, who are discontented with the slowness of their parents and are angry because the parents

would not run with their children, are considered disrespectful to their parents.

20 RNE: His devotion to the Motherland is so great that he would give his life for it, if necessary.

21 RNE: Our chief purpose is not to decry his work, but to believe that he is infinitely greater than we are, and to feel assured that compared with his work for India, ours is infinitesimal.

22 RNE: It is a bad habit to say that another man's thoughts are bad and ours only are good and that those holding different views from ours are the enemies of the country.

23 Allan Octavian Hume (1829–1912) and William Wedderburn (1838–1918): They were amongst those who formed the Indian National Congress in 1885.

24 RNE: I shall have to think the matter over. But what you say about Mr. Hume and Sir William Wedderburn is beyond my comprehension.

In both the 1909 and 1959 editions, હદ/हद is used, which broadly means limits/boundary. Gandhi suggests that when it comes to them, we should not exceed the boundaries of propriety.

25 Home Rule: 1909-GE: સ્વરાજ્ય (swarajya); 1959-HE: स्वराज्य.

26 Home Rule: 1909-GE: સ્વરાજ્ય (swarajya); 1959-HE: स्वराज्य.

27 RNE: To spend time over it is useless.
There is a difference between "passing time" and " spending time". The former is bereft of qualitative engagement, whereas the latter denotes a meaningful investment of time.

28 Home Rule: 1909-GE: સ્વરાજ્ય (swarajya); 1959-HE: स्वराज्य.

29 RNE: It is well that I should say unpleasant things at the commencement. It is my duty patiently to try to remove your prejudice.

30 Home Rule: 1909-GE: સ્વરાજ્ય (swarajya); 1959-HE: स्वराज्य.

31 Nation: 1909-GE: પ્રજા (praja); 1959-HE: प्रजा; Gandhi uses praja for people and "nation" throughout.

32 RNE: foretaste
33 RNE: nation
34 In Gujarati and Hindi, the sentence entails that the Congress should be used positively.

Chapter 2: The Partition of Bengal

1   The Partition of Bengal: 1909-GE: બંગાળાના ભાગલા (*Bangalana Bhagala*); 1959-HE: बंग-भंग.
2   Awakening: 1909-GE: જાગૃતિ (*Jagruti*); 1959-HE: जागृति.
3   RNE: At the time of the Partition, the people of Bengal reasoned with Lord Curzon, but in the pride of power he disregarded all their prayers. He took it for granted that Indians could only prattle, that they could never take any effective steps.
4   RNE: He used insulting language, and in the teeth of all opposition partitioned Bengal.
5   RNE: At that time feeling ran high.
6   RNE: They knew their power, hence the conflagration. It is now well-nigh unquenchable; it is not necessary to quench it either. The Partition will go, Bengal will be reunited, but the rift in the English barque will remain, it must daily widen.
7   RNE: The demand for the abrogation of the Partition is tantamount to a demand for Home Rule.
       In Gujarati and Hindi, the partition is abrogated, which means the partition of Bengal is annulled.
8   RNE: Hitherto we have considered that for redress of grievances we must approach the throne, and if we get no redress we must sit still, except that we may still petition.
       In Gujarati and Hindi, the throne is referred to as બાદશાહ/बादशाह (emperor). The throne can also be referred to as state power.
9   Force: 1959-GE: બળ (*Bal*); 1959:HE: ताक़त.

10 New spirit: 1909-GE: નવો જુસ્સો (*navo jusso*); 1959-HE: नया जोश; a new passion.

11 RNE: In the press: 1909-GE: છાપાના લખાણોમાં (*chhapana lakhanoma*)/ in print text; RNE: in the Press; 1959:HE- अख़बारों (newspapers).

12 RNE: awes

13 Sons of Soil: 1909-GE: હિંદના પુત્રરત્ન (*Hindna putraratna*); 1959:HE: हिन्द के पुत्ररत्न.

14 The spirit generated in Bengal has spread in the North to the Punjab, and, in the South, to Cape Comorin: 1909-GE: બંગાળાનો પવન ઉત્તરમાં પંજાબ લગી ને મદ્રાસ ઇલાકામાં કન્યાકુમારી ભૂશીર સુધી પહોંચી વળ્યો છે (The Bengal wind has crossed Punjab in the north and reached Kanyakamari Cape in Madras region); 1959-HE: बंगाल की हवा उत्तर में पंजाब तक और (दक्षिणमें) मद्रास इलाके में कन्याकुमारी तक पहुँच गई है।

15 RNE: Some call the Moderates the timid party, and the Extremists the bold party.

16 RNE: The one distrusts the other and imputes motives. At the time of the Surat Congress, there was almost a fight. I think that this division is not a good thing for the country, but I think also that such divisions will not last long.

Chapter 3: Discontent and Unrest

1 RNE: the Partition
2 RNE: So shall we be free from the present unrest which no one likes.
3 RNE: As long as a man is contented with his present lot, so long is it difficult to persuade him to come out of it.

Chapter 4: What is Swaraj?

1 RNE: I fear that our interpretation is not the same as yours.

2 Then we would understand that, in our language, the word "gone" is equivalent to "remained" : 1909-GE: તો પછી એમ માનશુ કે ગુજરાતી ભાષામાં "ગયા" એ શબ્દનો અર્થ કોઈ "રહ્યા" એમ કરે છે

RNE: Then we would understand that, in their language, the word "gone" is equivalent to "remained" ; 1959-HE: तब फिर हम ऐसा मानेंगे कि हमारी भाषा में कुछ लोग"जाना" का अर्थ रहना करते हैं.

3 RNE: Well then, let us suppose that the English have retired. What will you do then?

4 RNE: That question cannot be answered at this stage. The state after withdrawal will depend largely upon the manner of it. If, as you assume, they retire, it seems to me we shall still keep their constitution and shall carry on the Government. If they simply retire for the asking, we should have an army, etc, ready at hand. We should, therefore, have no difficulty in carrying on the Government.

5 RNE: Why do you want to drive away the English

6 Self-government: 1909-GE: રાજ્યસત્તા (*Rajyasatta*); RNE: Supposing we get Self-Government similar to what the Canadians and the South Africans have, will it be good enough; 1959-HE: राजसत्ता.

7 RNE: That question also is useless. We may get it when we have the same powers, we shall then hoist our own flag. As is Japan, so must India be. We must own our navy, our army, and we must have our own splendour, and then will India's voice ring through the world.

8 RNE: You have drawn the picture well.

9 RNE: You have drawn the picture well. In effect, it means this: that we want English rule without the Englishman. You want the tiger's nature, but not the tiger; that is to say, you would make India English. And when it becomes English, it will be called not Hindustan but *Englistan*.

10 RNE: If the education we have received be of any use, if the works of Spencer, Mill and others be of any importance, and if the English Parliament be the Mother of Parliaments, I certainly think that we should copy the English people, and this to such an extent that, just as they do not allow others to obtain a footing in their country, so we should not allow them or others to obtain it in ours.

11 There is need for patience:1909-GE: હજુ વાર (*Haju var chhe*/ there is still time); 1959-HE: अभी देर है.

12 RNE: I shall therefore, for the time being, content myself with endeavouring to show that what you call Swaraj is not truly Swaraj.

Chapter 5: The Condition of England

1 Sterile: 1909-GE: વાંઝણી (*Vanjhani*); 1959-HE: बाँझ.

2 RNE: That Parliament has not yet, of its own accord, done a single good thing. Hence I have compared it to a sterile woman.

3 RNE: The electors are considered to be educated and therefore we should assume that they would not generally make mistakes in their choice.

4 Effect: 1909-GE: અસર (*asar*); RNE: effects; 1959-HE: तेज.

5 Carlyle has called it the "talking- shop of the world" : 1909-GE: તેના એક મહાન લેખકે તેને "દુનિયાની વાતુડી" એવુ નામ આપ્યુ છે; 1959-HE: उसके एक महान लेखक ने उसे "दुनिया की बातूनी" जैसा नाम दिया है. In the Gujarati edition, his name is not mentioned. Gandhi refers to *Thomas Carlyle* (1881–1795) on several occasions. In *Autobiography,* he is referred to in the context of reading his book (*Heroes and Hero-worship),* panegyric on the Prophet. He also refers to him reading his book on the French Revolution (*CWMG IX*, 1963, p. 241). On the eve of elections for the legislative assembly under the Reforms of Act of 1919 to be held in November 1920, Gandhi gave "a humble

suggestion" in *Young India* (19 May 1920). "I observe that many candidates have come forward for the choice of the would-be electors for the reformed Councils. It must be granted that it is possible to render some service to the State by entering these Councils. But it is my firm belief that many can serve the country better by remaining outside. The late Mr. Keir Hardie used to say that it was practically impossible for a true Christian to remain in the British Parliament. Carlyle called it the talking shop" (*CWMG XVII*, 1965, p. 395). He also cites him during his "Speech at the Gandhi Seva Sangh Meeting", Hudli-II (17 April 1937). "Carlyle once said that members of the House of Commons had not much need of common sense" (*CWMG LXV*, 1976, p. 105).

6   RNE: If the money and the time wasted by Parliament were entrusted to a few good men, the English nation would be occupying to-day a much higher platform.

7   A true Christian: 1909-GE: ધર્મિષ્ટ માણસ (ધર્મિષ્ઠ માણસ-*Dharmiṣṭha manas*); 1959-HE: धर्मिष्ठ आदमी; religious person.

8   RNE: You have set me thinking, you do not expect me to accept at once all you say.

9   RNE: Parliament is without a real master. Under the Prime Minister, its movement is not steady, but it is buffeted about like a prostitute. The Prime Minister is more concerned about his power than about the welfare of Parliament . . . His care is not always that Parliament shall do right. Prime Ministers are known to have made Parliament do things merely for party advantage. All this is worth thinking over.

10   RNE: If they are to be considered honest because they do not take what are generally known as bribes, let them be so considered, but they are open to subtler influences.

11   RNE: As you express these views about Parliament,

12   Government: 1959-GE: સ્વરાજ્ય; 1959-HE: स्वराज्य; swarajya/swaraj.

13 The newspaper is considered a religious text. This is on par with the Bible, which is considered by devotees to be eternal. Herein, Gandhi highlights the close and unquestionable relationship between the two.

14 RNE: They take their cue from their newspapers which are often dishonest.

15 RNE: It is not due to any peculiar fault of the English people, but the condition is due to modem civilization. It is a civilization only in name.

Chapter 6: Civilisation

1 Civilisation: 1909-GE: સુધારાનું દર્શન; RNE: Throughout the chapter/book, civilisation changed as civilization; 1959-HE: सुधार का दर्शन.

2 In Gujarati, the sentence is a little longer: 1909-GE: હવે તો તમારે સુધારાની વાત પણ કરવી પડશે. તમારે હિસાબે તો સુધારો તે કુધારો થયો. The use of સુધારો (sudharo) and કુધારો (kudharo) is important; 1959-HE: अब तो आपको सुधार की भी बात करनी होगी. आपके हिसाब से तो सुधार बिगाड़ हुआ.

3 This is a book by Edward Carpenter. In the 1939 revised edition, when civilisation was changed to "civilization", the title of the book was also changed to "Civilization".

4 The object of life: In Gujarati and Hindi, the closest term is "aim of life", which is purusartha/purushartha in Hinduism. Purushartha has four aspects: *dharma, artha, kama,* and *moksa/moksha.* The concept has been read interconnectedly, critically, and in association with Gandhi. K. J. Shah emphasizes the interconnectedness of each component of Purushartha. "Artha will not be a *purusartha* unless it is in accord with *kama, dharma* and *moksa; kama* in turn will not be *kama* unless it is in accord with *dharma* and *moksa;* and *dharma* will not be *dharma,* unless it too is in accord with *moksa.* Equally *moksa* will not be *moksa* without the content of *dharma; dharma* will not be *dharma* without the content

of *kama* and *artha*. The four goals, therefore, constitute one single goal, though in the lives of individuals, the elements may get varying emphasis for various reasons" (Shah, 1992, p. 146).

Daya Krishna critically evaluates Purusharthas, "the myth of the purusartha". Originally, three goals were later expanded by the addition of moksa. There are certain ambiguities regarding linking and interpretation. "If we forget dharma, which is regarded as the distinctive feature of human beings distinguishing them from animals, and concentrate only on *artha* and *kama* for the present, we would discover that it is not very clear as to what is exactly meant by them. *Kama*, in the widest sense, may be understood as desire and, by implication, anything that is or can be the object of desire. But then everything will come under the category of kama, since obviously one can and does desire not only artha but even dharma and moksa. Such a use of the word kama is not so unwarranted as may seem at first sight." (Krishna, 1991, p. 189). Krishna also invites attention to ambiguities in defining purusharthas as descriptive or prescriptive. "Is it to be taken, for example, in a descriptive sense, that is, as describing what men actually pursue in their life? Or is it a prescriptive word which suggests what men ought to pursue in order to be worthy of being human? *Artha* and *kama* as examples of *purusarthas* tend to suggest the former, while *dharma* and *moksa* lead to the latter interpretation" (Krishna, 1991, p. 194). Citing the aforementioned quote from Shah, he complicates the concept of "only one single goal" and its relationship with four other goals. "[A]rtha is omitted... [while] ...talking of kama, and both artha and kama...[WHILE]...talking of dharma... What has *moksa* to do with *kama* and *artha*? Why does it have to relate to them only through the medium of *dharma*? Are *artha* and *kama* only contents, *dharma* both form and content, and *moksa* only pure form?" (Krishna, 1991, p. 203).

K.J. Shah states that "[t]he foundation of Gandhi's thought is the theory of *purushartha*" (Shah, 1996, p. 155). The unity of all existence is essential. He expresses *dharma, artha, kama* and *moksha* as discipline, wealth, power and pleasure. Under discipline, internal discipline concerning oneself and external discipline concerning others involve each other and are not independent. Regardless of the hierarchy within Purusharthas, the ultimate goal remains the same. Purushartha may appear to be a Hindu theory, but it may not be. "One can argue about discipline, wealth, power and pleasure independently of any specific form of because one of the modes of approach to the theory of *purushartha* is to be *loyal*, which is neither transcendental nor God-oriented" (Shah, 1996, p. 156).

Anthony Parel locates purushartha as the aim of life on any of the four accounts. "[I]t refers to any one of the four canonically recognised aims of life, viz., dharma (ethics and religion), artha (wealth and power), kama (pleasure), and moksha (liberation from samsara, the cycle of birth, death, and rebirth)" (Parel, 2007, p. 5). They become complementary to each other rather than overpowering, thus causing the path towards a "quest for harmony". For Parel, modern civilisation is based only on artha and kama while rejecting dharma and moksa. To promote world peace, we must combine all the basic ends of human life (Parel, 2015, pp. 137–155).

5   RNE: Formerly, they wore skins, and used spears as weapons.
6   RNE: steam engines
7   RNE: Formerly, only a few men wrote valuable books.
8   RNE: dished up
9   RNE: Formerly, men worked in the open air only as much as they liked.

10 RNE: Now thousands .

11 Dangerous occupations: 1909-GE: સીસા વિગેરેના (*sisa vagerena*/Lead etc) ; 1959-HE: सीसे वगैरह.

12 RNE: Formerly, men were made slaves under physical compulsion. Now they are enslaved by temptation of money and of the luxuries that money can buy.

13 RNE: This is a test of civilization. Formerly, special messengers were required and much expense was incurred in order to send letters, to-day, anyone can abuse his fellow by means of a letter for one penny. True, at the same cost, one can send one's thanks also. Formerly, people had two or three meals consisting of home-made bread and vegetables, now, they require something to eat every two hours so that they have hardly leisure for anything else.

14 RNE: half mad.

15 RNE: streets or they

16 RNE: This civilization is such that one has only to be patient and it will be self destroyed. According to the teaching of Mahomed this would be considered a Satanic Civilization Hinduism calls it the Black Age. I cannot give you an adequate conception of it. It is eating into the vitals of the English nation. It must be shunned Parliaments are really emblems of slavery. If you will sufficiently think over this, you will entertain the same opinion and cease to blame the English. They rather deserve our sympathy. They are a shrewd nation and I therefore believe that they will cast off the evil. They are enterprising and industrious and their mode of thought is not inherently immoral. Neither are they bad at heart. I therefore respect them. Civilization is not an incurable disease, but it should never be forgotten that the English people are at present afflicted by it.

Chapter 7: Why was India Lost?

1   RNE: If civilization is a disease and if it has attacked England, why has she been able to take India, and why is she able to retain it?

In Gujarati and Hindi editions, Angrej/English people is mentioned.

2   RNE: Swaraj, for

3   RNE: India, we

4   RNE: drinking *bhang*; Bhang: the cannabis plant's leaves.

5   RNE: disease, and if you

6   RNE Now I think

7   RNE: proceed further,

8   Nevertheless, I shall argue only when you will stop me: RNE: Nevertheless, I shall argue only when you stop me.

9   RNE: Princes

10   RNE: Some Englishmen state that they took and they hold India by the sword.

11   RNE: shop-keepers.

12   RNE: whether there was gold in the moon.

13   RNE: methods and get

14   RNE: same purpose and

15   RNE: Japan and not the Japanese.

16   RNE: The English have a treaty with Japan for the sake of their commerce, and you will see that if they can manage it their commerce will greatly expand in that country.

Chapter 8: The Condition of India

1   1909-GE: ઈંદુસ્તાનની દશા; 1959-HE: हिंदुस्तान की दशा- १.

2   હિંદુસ્તાનની અત્યારે રાંકડી દશા છે (*Hindustanani atyare rankaḍi dasha chhe*). आज हिंदुस्तान की रंक दशा हैं.

3   RNE: In thinking of it my eyes water and my throat gets parched.

4 RNE: heel, but
5 RNE: me and
6 RNE: lazy people and
7 RNE: and we therefore wish
8 RNE: Islam
9 RNE: worldly pursuits and
10 RNE: a similar strain, led
11 RNE: I am endeavouring to show to you
12 RNE: religion although
13 RNE: When its full effect is realised, we shall see that religious superstition is harmless compared to that of modern civilization. I am not pleading for a continuance of religious superstitions. We shall certainly fight them tooth and nail, but we can never do so by disregarding religion.
14 RNE: the Pax Britannica is a useless
15 1909-GE: ત્યારે તમે તો એમ પણ કહેશો કે ઇંગ્રેજે હીંદુસ્તાનમાં શાંતિનું સુખ આપ્યું છે તે નકામું છે (Then you will also say that the British brought about peace and happiness in India, which are useless); 1959-HE: तब तो आप यह भी कहेंगे कि अंग्रेजों ने हिंदुस्तान में शांति का जो सुख हमें दिया है वह बेकार है?
16 Thomas Babington Macaulay (1800–59) is widely known for his *Minutes on Education in India* (1935–37). He has invited a lot of criticism for his racist superiority. This is one of the most cited paragraphs, which has invited a slew of criticism:

"I have no knowledge of either Sanscrit or Arabic. But I have done what I could to form a correct estimate of their value. I have read translations of the most celebrated Arabic and Sanscrit works. I have conversed, both here and at home, with men distinguished by their proficiency in the Eastern tongues. I am quite ready to take the oriental learning at the valuation of the Orientalists themselves. I have never found one among them who could deny that a single shelf of a good European library was worth the whole native literature of India and Arabia. The intrinsic superiority of the Western literature is, indeed, fully admitted by those members of the committee who support the Oriental plan of education" (Macaulay, 1862, p. 107).

17 RNE: hardy mountaineers and infested

18 RNE: even to-day, but the English and you and I would hesitate to sleep where they sleep.

19 Home Rule: 1909: સ્વરાજ ; 1959-HE: स्वराज.

20 RNE: thugs

21 To conquer: 1909-GE: જીતવા (*Jitaval* to win); 1959-HE: जीतना ; It is important to note that "to conquer" entails "towards pursuance".

Chapter 9: The Condition of India (continued) Railways

1 1909-GE: હીંદુસ્તાનની દશા (ચાલુ): વિશેષ વિચાર (special thought); RNE: The Condition of India: Railways; 1959-HE- हिंदुस्तान की दशा—२ रेलगाड़ियाँ.

2 1909-GE: મોહ(moh/); 1959-HE: मोह; it may be translated as *infatuation.*

3 RNE: aspect, but when

4 RNE: dislike me because

5 RNE: country so much so that,

6 RNE: well, then I

7 RNE: the masses

8 RNE: famines because, owing

9 RNE: careless and so

10 RNE: Now-a-days rogues

11 RNE: nation before and

12 RNE: languages and there

13 RNE: farseeing

14 RNE: established Setubandha (Rameshwar) in the South, Jagannath in the East

15 RNE: And we Indians are one as no two Englishmen are

16 RNE: civilised as civilized throughout the text

17 This proverb is as follows: 1909-GE: મીયાંને ને મહાદેવને ન બને; 1959-HE: मियाँ और महादेव की नहीं बनेगी. This means "Muslims

and Hindus cannot get along". Gandhi cites this through the reader to reject this proposition, which was propagated along religious lines.

Chapter 10: The Condition of India (continued). The Hindus and the Mahomedans

1 1909-GE: હિંદુસ્તાનની દશા-(ચાલુ) હિંદુ-મુસલમાન; 1959-GE: हिंदुस्तान की दशा -३ हिंदू- मुसलमान.

2 RNE: Man abused it so

3 RNE: immediate neighbours, but in my conceit I

4 RNE: Owing to them, man has gone further away from his Maker.

5 Mahomedanism: 1909-GE: મુસલમાન/Muslim ; 1959-HE: मुसलमानों/Muslims.

6 RNE: nation; they

7 RNE: fellow countrymen

8 RNE: unity, if only

9 RNE: terms; nor

10 RNE: sovereigns and

11 RNE: With the English advent quarrels recommenced.

12 RNE: were fighting, to

13 RNE: roads so

14 RNE: Jainism; but

15 RNE: enslaved and,

16 RNE: cow-protection

17 RNE: The cow is the protector of India because, being an agricultural country, she is dependent on the cow. The cow is a most useful animal in hundreds of ways.

18 RNE: a cow no

19 RNE: In doing so, I would become an enemy of the Mahomedan as well as of the cow.

20 RNE: save her but

21 RNE: If I put on superior air, he will return the compliment.

22 RNE: more so; and if

23 Blood-brother: 1909-GE: મારો ભાઈ (maro bhai/ my brother); 1959-HE: मेरा भाई.

24 RNE: Who ever

25 RNE: Lastly, if it be true that the Hindus believe in the doctrine of non-killing and the Mahomedans do not, what, pray, is the duty of the former?

26 RNE: Ahimsa

27 RNE: Ahimsa

28 RNE: Ahimsa

29 RNE: Ahimsa

30 These thoughts are put into our minds by selfish and false religious teachers: Gandhi is very bold and critical in Gujarati. 1909-GE: આવા વિચારો સ્વાર્થી ધર્મશિક્ષક, શાસ્ત્રીઓ, મુલ્લાંઓએ આપ્યા છે/Selfish religious teachers, scribes (*shastris*), and mullahs have imparted such ideas to us; 1959-HE: ऐसे विचार स्वार्थी धर्म शिक्षकों, शास्त्रियों और मुल्लाओं ने हमें दिए हैं.

31 RNE: writing history, they

32 RNE: We in our ignorance then fall at their feet

33 RNE: Those who do not wish to misunderstand things may read up the Koran, and they will find hundreds of passages acceptable to the Hindus; and the *Bhagavad-gita* contains passages to which not a Mahomedan can take exception.

34 Gandhi's interest in the Gita, reading, interpretation, shaping the nationalist discourse, the question of justice for historical and bodily injustice, and method have all prompted critical scrutiny.

Gandhi references the Gita in Satyagraha as a source of unborrowable courage. Courage cannot be borrowed. "A man cannot borrow faith or courage from others. The doubter is marked out for destruction, as the Gita puts it. My faith and courage were at their highest in Tolstoy Farm" (Gandhi, 1928, p. 371). For Gandhi, as per the Gita, there is no distinction between pleasure and pain, victory and defeat (Gandhi, 1928, p. 394).

In 1889, he encountered Sir Edwin Arnold's *Song Celestial,* an English translation of the Bhagavad Gita. Gandhi elaborates on his encounter with the Gita in an unusual way in his autobiography. "Towards the end of my second year [1889] in England, I came across two theosophist brothers, both unmarried. They talked to me about the Gita. They were reading Sir Edwin Arnold's translation—*The Song Celestial*—and they invited me to read the original with them. I felt ashamed, as I had read the divine poem neither in Samskriti nor in Gujarati" (Gandhi, 2018, pp. 145–46). He also tried to unify the teachings of the Gita, *the Light of Asia, or the Great Renunciation (Mahabhinishkramana), Being the Life and Teaching of Gautama* by Edwin Arnold, and *Sermon on the Mount.* The Gita's implications for him were ideas of trusteeship, jurisprudence, non-possession, and equability, presupposing a change of heart and equipoise to act without desiring the fruit (Gandhi, 2018). Gandhi also cites verses from the Bhagavad Gita to highlight desire-led implications, one of which is task-led implications.

Concerning the meaning of the Gita or method of reading the text, in 1925, he stated that "[f]or understanding the meaning of the Shastras, one must have a well-cultivated moral sensibility and experience in the practice of their truths" (*CWMG XXVIII*, 1968, p. 316). He also added that "any interpretation of a Shastra that is opposed to truth cannot be right" (*CWMG XXVIII*, 1968, p. 317). Moreover, spirit and meaning in the total context are more important than literal interpretation (*CWMG XXVIII*, 1968, p. 318). Non-violence is at the core of the Gita. "If, moreover, it is difficult to reconcile a few of the verses with the idea that the Gita advocates non-violence, it is still more difficult to reconcile the teaching of the greater as a whole with the advocacy of violence" (*CWMG XXVIII*, 1968, p. 318).

Gandhi gave talks on the Gita between 24 February and 26 November 1926, at Satyagraha Ashram, Ahmedabad. Mahadev Desai and Punjabhai noted these talks. Narahari Parikh edited and published it as *Gandhijinu Gitashiksham* in 1955 (*CWMG XXXII*, 1969, p. 94). The introduction offers a unique perspective on the text. Gandhi emphasizes the importance of freedom from attachment and aversion in his introductory talks, reframing the Gita as a battle between virtue and vice. Notably, he did not discuss violence and non-violence, focusing instead on the text's purpose: to guide man in his inner strife (*CWMG XXXII*, 1969, p. 95).

Gandhi's reading of the Gita as a non-violent text is not without question.

"When I was in London, I had talks with many revolutionaries. Shyamji Krishnavarma, [V.D.] Savarkar and others used to tell me that the Gita *and* the *Ramayana* taught quite the opposite of what I said they did. When even highly learned and thoughtful men read this meaning in the Gita, what can we expect of ordinary people?" (*CWMG XXXII*, 1969, p. 102). The text uses the battle as a pretext to emphasize morality and great truths. In terms of decisions, relationships do not matter. This is an ignorant distinction. He also cites Raychandbhai's maxim: "Accept innocent happiness, innocent joy, whatever the source" (*CWMG XXXII*, 1969, p. 105). Doing away with "I" is essential for self-realisation. "The chief aim of the epic, however, is to represent the most invisible of all invisible wars. The moral problems that confront one in this inner war are far more difficult than those of a physical war" (*CWMG XXXII*, 1969, p. 108). Gandhi asserts that the Gita does not make any decisions for us. However, when "faced with a moral problem, you give up attachment to the ego and then decide what you should do, you will come to no harm. This is the substance of the argument that Shri Krishna has explained into 18 chapters" (*CWMG XXXII*, 1969, p. 109). Gandhi reads about the limitations of our senses and urges us to go beyond them. Fear is the cause of killing, and those who are not afraid of death do not kill. Gandhi suggests that all castes and genders can read the text. He links possessiveness with violence. The former is a prerequisite for the latter. "Where there is potential, there is violence" (*CWMG XXXII*, 1969, p. 115). The principle of collective possession becomes important when individual possession is restricted to the minimum level. The path of action is essential. Where self-interest is a driving force, action without expectation is not appropriate. In this debate, he also highlights the significance of 'means'. In terms of action and outcome, attachment poses a significant obstacle. He cites the following from the verse: "Work without attachment, being established firmly in yoga. Yoga means renouncing the fruit of action. It means not desiring the fruit of work, which is *akarma*" (*CWMG XXXII*, 1969, p. 125). Does Gandhi pose that attachment to good work as a problem? He points out that "[i]f we are attached to our goal of winning swaraj, we shall not hesitate to adopt bad means" (*CWMG XXXII*, 1969, p. 125). The concept of non-attachment is rooted in Anasakti Yoga.

Sthitaprajna (steady wisdom, calm, or "one who is of steadfast intellect") is another component of the significant value. "He who banishes all bad desires arising in his mind may be described as a *sthitaprajna*" (*CWMG XXXII*, 1969, p. 128). Gandhi also adds that "[h]e whose self abides content in itself is known as *sthitaprajna*" (*CWMG XXXII*, 1969, p. 128). Means and ends should become one. This is the path towards firmness of mind. The cultivation of firmness of mind is an essential criterion for satyagraha. Concern for others becomes important. "The world's night is our day, and the world's day is our night" (*CWMG XXXII*, 1969, p. 143). Herein, *naishkarmya* (freedom from experiencing the results of action) does not mean refusal to work. Refusal to work does not lead to the experience of *naishkarmya* (*CWMG XXXII*, 1969, p. 148). Karma refers to any bodily or motional action. Easing karma is not possible. He also links Gita to practical life concerns. "A dharma that does not serve practical needs is no dharma; it is *adharma*" (*CWMG XXXII*, 1969, p. 152). *Yajna* is sacrificing without making others suffer. Yajna means "any action performed with a view of public good" (*CWMG XXXII*, 1969, p. 155). For Gandhi, "the right *yajna* for this age is the *yajna* of spinning" (*CWMG XXXII*, 1969, p. 159). Linking yajna and labour, he defines labour as bodily labour while referring to the Russian author Bondoref's notion of bread labour. "He alone should eat who has laboured for twelve hours" (*CWMG XXXII*, 1969, p. 159). Furthermore, "he is a thief who does not do bodily labour for society" (*CWMG XXXII*, 1969, p. 160). Bodily labour is part of yajna in the form of sacrifice. Furthermore, there is a need to "give up the ways of masters and turn ourselves into workers. If, while working as labourers, we learn to be detached and make ourselves cyphers, we would come out of the darkness of night" (*CWMG XXXII*, 1969, p. 162). The yajna depicts this. The spinning wheel is our age's supreme yajna. Yajna is an activity for the good of others (*CWMG XXXII*, 1969, p. 163). Work is the core of *yajna*. "*Laborare est orare*—Work is worship" (*CWMG XXXII*, 1969, p. 164). A non-violent person is free from attachment and aversion (*CWMG XXXII*, 1969, pp. 178–79).

Gandhi also invites attention to satyagraha and love. "We can offer Satyagraha only against a person who has some love in his heart. We can control another only if there is mutual love between us; where there is no such love, the only course for us is non-cooperation with the other party" (*CWMG XXXII*, 1969, p. 182). Non-violence makes violence disappear (*CWMG XXXII*, 1969, p. 193).

He explains the significance of civil disobedience, law and outlaws. Outlaw is intentional, which is the core of civil disobedience. "Even a thief has to submit to the law. He is not a rebel. The person who defies a law with a deliberate intention to do so is an outlaw. We become outlaws when we commit civil disobedience, for our disobedience is deliberate. Those who commit civil disobedience and do so deliberately are also outlaws, but the person who steals in abject helplessness is still ruled by the country's law" (*CWMG XXXII*, 1969, pp. 196–97).

Gandhi emphasizes the significance of an act of labour through his commentary. Physical labour has become extremely important. Yoga is a "skill in action". Cultivating self-control is another vital suggestion. *Sanyaasi* is not a branch of *karamyoga,* and *sanyaasa* and karamyoga *are* delinked. Gandhi also defines the meaning of *sannyasi* as the absence of attachments, aversions, and "I". "He who has become free from attachments and aversions, who has shed the "I" in him, has become a true sannyasi" (*CWMG XXXII*, 1969, p. 225). The debate on "I" is pertinent for self and other, or swaraj, where other is very much part of self. On "I", he says that "we can thus take it as a mathematical truth that our work will tend to evil in proportion as we are conscious of the 'I' in us, and it will tend to good in proportion as we shed that 'I'" (*CWMG XXXII*, 1969, p. 226).

Equal regard for others is a feature of *samadarshi.* Samadarshi is "the one who gives to each according to his or her need" (*CWMG XXXII*, 1969, p. 231). There will be food for the enemy first, and hatred for the enemy will be discarded. Against this backdrop, he also defines the rule of swadeshi: serving the people near us (physically) and distant from us (mentally). In other words, the enemies, whether near physically or away mentally, should be served first (*CWMG XXXII*, 1969, p. 232).

Yoga also entails the absence of suffering (*CWMG XXXII*, 1969, p. 247). Gandhi compares the spinning wheel with the *unmanifest*. He also adds that treating the visible universe as illusory is beyond reason. The renunciation of the fruits of action is nothing but freeing oneself from attachment and ego. He also subjects *the shastras* to the test of truth and non-violence. In its absence, it may lead to a fall. For Gandhi, both the concept of Swaraj and its methods hold significance. Gandhi suggests that the book is for all people, irrespective of faith, and that this is the book of pure ethics. Karma is the body, and we cannot live without it. Seeing the body means seeing karma. It is an act. Karma is also violence. Thus, complete freedom from karma, or violence, is moksha, or salvation. It also means the obliteration of "I" (*CWMG XXXII*, 1969, pp. 301–56).

Gandhi also published a simplified version of "Discourses on the Gita" for ordinary readers from Yeravada jail upon being found difficult by an ashram member at the time of publication. Amidst the series of letters, a letter was devoted to each chapter of the Gita in a simplified language. This simplified *Discourse on* the Gita was translated by Valji Govindhi Desai into English (Desai, 1960, p. 4).

Gandhi also wrote about the Gita in *Young India* on 6 August 1931. Herein, he offers a slew of significant interpretations. Here, he also does not consider the Mahabharata a historical work. The author of the Mahabharata highlights the futility of physical warfare in place of the necessity of physical warfare. Victors inherit the legacy of misery. In it, the Gita is the crown. Self-realization is the renunciation of the fruits of action. Action is a must, not an attachment, which causes "I". Renunciation is not indifference to the result. Actions towards the result, irrespective of the outcome of the result, are interpreted as renouncing the fruits of the result. "Renunciation means the absence of hankering after fruit" (Gandhi, 1931, p. 207). He does see the dichotomy between salvation and worldly pursuits. He explicates the animals and work-like conditions in the text. "But is the Gita believed in *Ahimsa* or was it included in desirelessness? Why did the author take a warlike illustration? When the Gita was written, although people believed in *Ahimsa*, wars were not only taboo, but nobody observed the contradiction between them and *Ahimsa*" (Gandhi, 1931, p. 207).

This message is presented as "*Anasaktiyoga: The message of the Gita*" in the volume edited by Mahadev Desai, The Gospel of Selfless Action, or the Gita according to Gandhi (Desai, 1946).

Gandhi's commentary and interpretations have attracted considerable attention.

Robert Charles Zaehner (1966) offers an exciting analysis of Gandhi, a slew of his actions and Hinduism. "The outraged conscience of Yudhishthira speaks through the lips of Mahatma Gandhi. And Gandhi's God is the God of Yudhishthira, not the God of bhakti or philosophers. 'To me, God is Truth and Love; God is ethics and morality, God is fearlessness; God is the source of Light and Life, and yet he is above and beyond all these. God is conscience.' God is, in fact, what Gandhi in his heart feels him to be: he is not the God of the law books or even of the Vedas, should these prove to conflict with the light within him" (Zaehner, 1966, pp. 171–72). Moreover, "Gandhi did not let Hinduism go; but after Gandhi, Hinduism will never be the same again" (Zaehner, 1966, p. 185).

Dipesh Chakrabarty and Rochona Majumdar (2013, 66–87) link the Gita in the context of *satyagrahis*. "The aim of reading and discussing the Gita daily was to transform the text into the *satyagrahi's* talisman. There was no longer a project of "purifying" politics. Rather, the project was constantly to purify, and thus shield the self of the satyagrahi who entered the political fray as part of necessary action in life. This, we may say, was Gandhi's way of accepting politics as it actually was" (Chakrabarty & Majumdar, 2013, pp. 70–71). The first strategy in Gandhi's reading of the Gita was to treat the text as an allegory. This helped him examine his inner self. It was an anti-history move (Chakrabarty & Majumdar, 2013, pp. 79–80).

For Faisal Devji, "the task Gandhi set himself in his interpretation of the Bhagavad-Gita was not to avoid action, or even its inevitable violence, but to attend upon its very materiality in a sort of phenomenology" (Devji, 2012, p. 100).

J.T.F. Jordens pays closer attention to Gandhi's interpretation and ommission from the text as well as his diversion and conversion with traditional interpreters. Regarding the diversion, "Gandhi's approach to the *Gita* differs markedly from the method of many traditional interpreters who expend great effort on textual interpretation and on establishing the internal logic of the various theoretical statements and practical directives of the text" (Jordens, 1986, p. 109). However, concerning convergence, "in one important way, Gandhi's approach is in close conformity with a major traditional rule of interpretation. He identifies the central, key passage in the text: the *mahavakya*, "the great statement" that gives the central message, in terms of which all the rest of the text must be explained. For Gandhi, the last twenty stanzas of Chapter Two constitute the Gita's *mahavakya* in the description of the *sthitaprajna* (Jordens, 1986, p. 109).

Nagappa Gowda also emphasizes that, for Gandhi, the Gita is a text on non-violence. Gandhi read from some of the other readings, like Bankim or Tilak. For them, "although the Gita justified non-violence, in the final analysis it substantially supported violence on ethical grounds. Aurobindo went far beyond them and argued that the Gita was basically a text on violence and not non-violence, as he believed violence to be a natural and innate aspect of the universal project of emancipation" (Gowda, 2011, p. 147). Gandhi makes the truth a universal domain, transcending the boundaries of history to decipher the meaning of the text. This is also true in the context of *Hind Swaraj*. "One of the significant positions that Gandhi takes in his writings, and particularly in *Hind Swaraj*, is that for acquiring objective knowledge of a moral subject, one is not expected to concentrate attention on tracing its internal histories, its origins and processes of evolution and growth, because these facts would neither change the truth nor would they add to it, and hence, they have nothing to do with the truth of an object or a text. Truth is absolute, unchanging and universal; history has not touched it, nor can it ever do so in the future. The "truth", which guides human beings at all times to deliver them from the bondage of karma and leads them to moral life, cannot be based on historical explanation. Such a truth always remains outside and beyond the purview of history. Hence, the validation of truth does not lie in its historical demonstrations; such efforts are futile in the pursuit of truth" (Gowda, 2011, p. 172). Due to this, Gandhi also rejects "the Vedico-Puranic theory of avatar", calling it unrealistic imagination. The central thrust of reading the Gita is anasakti, which is rationalistic against the former version, which relies on avatara (Gowda, 2011, p. 182). Gandhi's take on varna, as present in Gita, has invited multidimensional criticism. Gowda offers anasakti as the entry point for this. "However, the emphasis here too was not so much on the intrinsic goodness of the institution of varna but its access to anasakti" (Gowda, 2011, p. 195). "Gandhi felt that the community of anasaktas would constitute role models for the masses. However, such a community would be inclusive and nonhierarchical and put the ethics of anasakti into practice" (Gowda, 2011, p. 199).

35 RNE: on me; and, similarly,
36 RNE: counsels we
37 RNE: clay pot
38 RNE: danger-point
39 RNE: numbers; they pretend that they are more educated;
40 RNE: not equitable; In Gujarati and Hindi, મતિના and अकल are used. મતિ or अकल entail intellect, intelligence, or understanding.
41 RNE: But when
42 RNE: men fight, both

Chapter 11: The Condition of India (continued)
Lawyers

1 1909-GE: ઈંદુસ્તાનની દશા (ચાલુ) વકીલ-દાક્તર); 1959-HE: हिंदुस्तान की दशा – ४ वकील.
2 RNE: when two men quarrel they
3 My firm opinion is that the lawyers have enslaved India, have accentuated Hindu-Mahomedan dissensions and have confirmed English authority.
4 Manmohan Ghose/Manomohan Ghose/Monomohun Ghose (1844–96) was founder of the *Indian Mirror* (1861). He was the first Indian barrister-at-law at Calcutta High Court in 1867. He was active in the Indian Association and was a delegate to England (1885). He was active in the Indian National Congress (Seal, 1971, p. 382). He, along with others, "strongly opposed to...a double standard of education for

males and females" (Kopf, 1979, p. 124). Gandhi refers to him while establishing reasoning between legal talent and honesty. "I do not believe for one moment that legal talent has to be bought if it is to remain honest. I recall the names of Motilal Nehru, C.R. Das, Manomohan Ghose, Badruddin Tyabji and a host of others, who gave their legal talent absolutely free of charge and served their country faithfully and well. The taunt may be flung in my face that they did so because they were able to charge princely fees in their own professional work. I reject that argument, for the simple reason that I have known every one of them with the exception of Manomohan Ghosh...I can point our to you several lawyers of distinction who, if they had not come to the national cause, would today be occupying seats on the High Court Benches in all parts of India" (*CWMG XLVIII*, 1971, p. 218).

5   RNE: all about it; he
6   RNE: But they go to lawyers.
7   RNE: do not do so the
8   RNE: quarrels instead of
9   RNE: wealthy and their
10 RNE: will charge and
11 RNE: ruined through them, they
12 Principalities: 1909-GE: ૨૪વાડી; 1959-GE: रियासत.
13 RNE: the lawyers"
14 RNE: Governments
15 It is used for cowardly.
16 decide for
17 RNE: less so, if
18 RNE: without lawyers courts could not have been established or conducted and
19 RNE: profession, and consider
20 RNE: cousins; and

Chapter 12: The Condition of India (continued)
Doctors

1 1909-GE: હિંદુસ્તાનની દશા -- (ચાલુ)દાક્તર; 1958-HE: हिंदुस्तान की दशा – ५ डॉक्टर.

2 Hateful: 1909-GE: કનિષ્ઠ; 1959-HE: कनिष्ठ; કનિષ્ઠ/કનિષ્ઠ entails junior; In Gujarati, hateful is દ્વેષભર્યું (*dveṣabharyu*; a hateful remark); કનિષ્ઠ is junior or younger or with little experience.

3 Poisonous tree/Antiaris toxicaria.

4 RNE: my mind but represent

5 RNE: by me and I would not have overeaten again.

6 RNE: more at ease;

7 RNE: freed from vice and

8 RNE: their bodies, and

9 All say that it is not necessary to take so many lives for the sake of our bodies: 1909-GE: હિંદુ, મુસલમાન, ખ્રિસ્તી, પારસી બધા કહે છે કે માણસના શરીરને સારુ આટલા જીવો મારવાની જરૂર નથી; 1959-HE: हिंदु, मुसलमान, ईसाई, जरथोस्ती— सब धर्म कहते हैं कि आदमी के शरीर के लिए इतने जीवों को मारने की जरूरत नहीं; Both means: *Hindus, Muslims, Christians, Parsis all say that it is not necessary to kill so many creatures for the sake of human bodies.*

10 worth a few pennies, cost shillings: It's important to understand that doctors overcharge for minimal services.

11 RNE: populace, in

Chapter 13: What is True Civilisation?

1 1909-GE: ખરો સુધારો શું?; 1959-HE: सच्चा सुधार कौन सा?

2 *typo*: ancesters

3 RNE: Rome went, Greece shared the same fate; the might of the Pharaohs was broken; Japan has become Westernised; of China nothing can be said; but India is still, somehow or other, sound at the foundation.

4   RNE: her beauty: it
5   Added: *The Gujarati equivalent for civilisation means "good conduct."*
6   RNE: our passions the
7   RNE: as existed
8   RNE: former times and
9   RNE: They, therefore,
10 RNE: and that people would not be happy in them, that there would be gangs of thieves and robbers, prostitution and vice flourishing in them and that poor men would be robbed by rich men.
11 RNE: people, they
12 RNE: independently and
13 RNE: railways and to
14 RNE: girls dedicate themselves to prostitution, and in the name of religion sheep and goats are killed.
15 RNE: Attempts have always been made and will be made to remove them.
16 RNE: civilization, as described by me, has
17 RNE: The tendency of the Indian civilization is to elevate the moral being, that of the Western civilization is to propagate immorality.

Chapter 14: How Can India Become Free?

1   1909-GE: હિંદ કેમ છૂટે? ; 1959:HE- हिन्द कैसे आज़ाद हो? In a substantive sense, both mean "How does India become free?"
2   RNE: indirectly, we
3   RNE: Western
4   RNE: Yet
5   RNE: There is no
6   RNE: The Swaraj that I wish to picture is such that, after we have once realized it, we shall endeavour to the end of our lifetime to persuade others to do likewise. But such Swaraj has to be experienced, by each one for himself.

7   RNE: Others will leave of their own accord.

8   One of our poets says that slaves cannot even dream of happiness: In both Gujarati and Hindi editions, a couplet from Indian poet Tulsidas" Ramcharitmanas is quoted; 1909-GE:પરાધીન સપને સુખી નહિ; 1959-HE: पराधीन सपने सुखनाही.

In Ramcharitmanas, the full couplet is:

कत बिधि सृजीं नारि जग माहीं। पराधीन सपनेहूँ सुखु नाहीं॥
भै अति प्रेम बिकल महतारी। धीरजु कीन्ह कुसमय बिचारी॥

(Ramcharitmanas, 2022, p. 116)

In Hindi:

विधाता ने जगत में स्त्री जाति को क्यों पैदा किया? पराधीन को सपने में भी सुख नहीं मिलतायों कहती हुई माता प्रेम में अत्यन्त विकल हो गयी, परन्तु कुसमय जानकर (दुःख करने का अवसर न जानकर) उन्होंने धीरज धरा (Ramcharitmanas, 2022, p. 116).

In F.S. Growse's English translation in 1914, it is as follows: "Why has God created woman in the world, seeing that she is always in a state of subjection, and never can even dream of happiness? Though utterly distracted by motherly love, she knew it was no time to display it, and restrained herself" (Growse, 1914, p. 69). Growse translates *paradhin* as "a state of subjection".

Philip Lutgendorf translates this in the following manner:

Oh Why did Brahma make women in the world- always subservient and deprived of happiness?

Though overwhelmed by love, her mother composed herself, mindful of the moment (Lutgendorf, 2016, p. 211).

Lutgendorf uses subservient for paradhin.

Gandhi picks up "पराधीन सपनेहूँ सुखु नाहीं"for rephrasing and universalising it. The contextual use was rephrased for universal cause that is a struggle against imperialism. In this the translation of पराधीन सपनेहूँ सुखु नाहीं suggests "the subjected person does not get happiness, even in dreams".

9   Typo in RNE as Reader.

10 RNE: What was possible for Mazzini and Garibaldi, is possible for us

11 Great men: 1909-GE: મહાવીર ; 1959-HE: महावीर; Gandhi accords "great men" status based on both principle and action, i.e., "act based on principle".

Chapter 15: Italy and India

1   Gandhi read Giuseppe Mazzini/Joseph Mazzini (1805–72) for India's freedom in a non-binary manner. Gandhi wrote "Joseph Mazzini: A Remarkable Career" in 1905 (*Indian Opinion*, 22 July 1905). He said, "[b]efore 1870 Italy comprised a number of small principalities, each with its petty chief. Before 1870, she was like the India or Kathiawad of today...Today Italy is an independent European country and her people are regarded as a distinct nation. All this can be said to be the achievement of one man. And his name—Joseph Mazzini...He was a man of such sterling character, so good-natured and so patriotic, that great preparations are being made throughout Europe to commemorate the centenary of his birth...[H]e was so broadminded that he could be regarded [as] a citizen of every country. It was his constant yearning that every nation should become great and live in unity...The sufferings of others he regarded as his own. There are very few instances in the world where a single man has brought about the uplift of his country by his strength of mind and his extreme devotion during his own lifetime. Such was

the unique Mazzini" (*CWMG V*, 1961, pp. 27–28). In 1907, he wrote that "[t]he great patriot Mazzini used to say that it was to his country that he was married" (*CWMG VII*, 1962, p. 14).

2   RNE: man, Garibaldi;
   Giuseppe Garibaldi (1807–82) is known for his contribution to Italian unification.

3   RNE: Mazzini's ambition was not and has not yet been realised regarding Italy

4   How to rule himself: 1909-GE: સ્વરાજ્ય (swaraj); 1959-HE: स्वराज्य.

5   RNE: If you believe that because Italians rule Italy the Italian nation is happy, you are groping in darkness.

6   RNE: kings with the

7   RNE: They, therefore,

8   RNE: one thing, how can the millions obtains self-rule?

9   RNE: the English, and if you

10   RNE: princes if only

11   RNE: armed, that

12   RNE: civilization, and if that

13   RNE: can and so

14   You are over-stating the facts. All need not be armed. At first, we shall assassinate a few Englishmen and strike terror; then, a few men who will have been armed will fight openly. We may have to lose a quarter of a million men, more or less, but we shall regain our land. We shall undertake guerilla warfare, and defeat the English.

15   RNE: to sacrifice ourselves

16   RNE: thought, that

17   RNE: and other similar acts

18   RNE: England

Chapter 16: Brute-Force

1   1909-GE: દારૂ ગોળી (*darugolo*/ammunition);RNE: BRUTE
       FORCE; 1959-HE: गोला-बारूद; Brute force is very much present
       in most of the writers on civilisation. It is contrasted against
       ethical practice or non-violence.

2   RNE: new doctrine, that

3   RNE: simple-minded its

4   RNE: recommence

5   RNE: things and they

6   RNE: may receive we

7   RNE: Somehow or other, we

8   RNE: brute force and that it is possible for us to do likewise,
       but by using similar means

9   RNE: distorted and men

10   RNE: worship God; it

11   RNE: I do not wish to imply that they do no duties. They
       don" t perform the duties corresponding to those rights; and
       as they do not perform that particular duty namely, acquire
       fitness, their rights have proved a burden to them.

12   RNE: it, if I

13   RNE: If it is my father who has come to steal I shall use one
       kind of means. If it is an acquaintance I shall use another; and
       in the case of a perfect stranger I shall use a third.

14   RNE: say you will

15   RNE: top to toe; "from head to toe . . . from head to
       heels or foot; from tip or top to toe. Over the entire body,
       in its entirety... These expressions date from ancient times.
       The alliterative head to heels originated about 1400, and
       Shakespeare had "from top to toe" in Hamlet (1:2)" (Ammer,
       2013, p. 158).

16   RNE: armed and I

17   RNE: anger and we

18 RNE: I therefore hesitate to
19 RNE: For the time being I
20 RNE: it is clear you will
21 RNE: That well armed man has stolen your property; you
    have harboured the thought of his act, you are filled with
    anger; you argue that you want to punish that rogue, not for
    your own sake, but for the good of your neighbours; you have
    collected a number of armed men, you want to take his house
    by assault; he is duly informed of it, he runs away; he too is
    incensed.
22 RNE: brother robbers
23 RNE: him you
24 RNE: They complain before you. You reply that you are
    doing all for their sake, you do not mind that your own goods
    have been stolen.
25 It involves selecting the lesser of two evils. Homer's *The
    Odyssey* contains the vivid reference to Scylla and Charybdis.
    "We then sailed on up the narrow strait with wailing. For
    on one side lay Scylla and on the other divine Charybdis..."
    (Homer,1919, p. 449). "Now when we had escaped the rocks,
    and dread Charybdis and Scylla, presently then we came to
    the goodly island of the god, where were the fair kine, broad
    of brow, and the many goodly flocks of Helios Hyperion"
    (Homer, 1919, p. 451).
26 RNE: grows, the
27 RNE: opportunity: you argue man, you
28 RNE: a fellow man, you
29 RNE: open, you
30 RNE: The robber comes again and is confused as all this is
    new to him;
31 RNE: Thus, you see, different means
32 RNE: but I only wish to show that fair means alone can
    produce fair results, and that, at least m the majority of cases,

if not indeed in all, the force of love and pity is infinitely greater than the force of arms.

33 RNE: their condition and warn

34 RNE: We shall hurt

35 RNE: we shall be no longer

36 The force implied in this may be described as love-force, soul-force or, more popularly but less accurately, passive resistance: 1909-GE:આ બળ તે દયા બળ કહો, આત્મબળ કહો, સત્યાગ્રહ કહો; 1959-HE: "इस बल को चाहे दया बल कहें, चाहे आत्मबल कहें या सत्याग्रह कहें. Love force/દયાબળ/दयाबल, soul-force/આત્મબળ/आत्मबल, and passive resistance/સત્યાગ્રહ/सत्याग्रह are used to make more impact.

37 1909-GE: એક નનો છત્રિસ રોગને હરે: RNE: One negative cures thirty six diseases; 1959-HE: एक नाही सब रोगो की दवा. It means that one "no" cures all diseases ("one negative" cures all diseases).

38 RNE: own life because

39 RNE: In using brute force against the English you consult entirely your own, that is the national, interest.

40 RNE: If you say that the actions of the English, being evil, represent fire, and that they proceed to their actions through ignorance, and that therefore they occupy the position of a child and that you want to protect such a child, then you will have to overtake every evil action of that kind by whomsoever committed and, as in the case of the evil child, you will have to sacrifice yourself.

Chapter 17: Passive Resistance

1 1909-GE: સત્યાગ્રહ- આત્મબળ (satyagraha- atmabaḷa); 1959-HE: सत्याग्रह– आत्मबल.

2 RNE: religion, pity, or love, is

3 1909:GE: દયા ધરમ કો મુલ હય, દેહ મુલ અભિમાન; તુલસી દયા ન છાંડીએ, જબ લગ ઘટ મે પ્રાન. (*Daya dharamako mool*

hai, deha mool abhiman; tulsi daya na chhaṇḍiye, jab lag ghaṭ me prana);

Gandhi uses *deh mool* over *paap mool*.
The original couplet is:

"दया धर्म को मूल है, पाप मूल अभिमान।
तुलसी दया न छांडिए, जब लगि घट में प्राना॥"

Gandhi's shift from sin (*paap*) to body (*deh*) is discernible.

This couplet is considered popularly attributed to Tulisdas (Parel, 1997, p. 88), and is a part of the folk tradition of north India (Sharma & Suhrud, 2010, p. 72).

Mrityunjay, a noted critic (CSDS, Delhi), offers a pertinent observation. According to him, Gandhi has used this couplet (*dohe*) in *Hind Swaraj*. This is considered to be a couplet of Tulsidas because the name of the creator is mentioned in the couplet as "Tulsi" (तुलसी दया न छांडिए/ Do not leave kindness, Tulsi). However, this couplet is not found in any of Tulsi's books present or survived in the written format. It is possible that this couplet may have come from folk tradition *(lok parampara)*. Since medieval literature was based on the *Shruti tradition* (the Shruti tradition is based on hearing*)*, popular folk or other writers" works frequently rose to fame under the pen names of well-known writers. Popular verses known by Kabir's name serve as real-world examples. Citing that couplet, scholars have stated that the word "sin" was present in the original folk tradition rather than "deh". Gandhi used the word "deh" rather than "sin". This comprehension is divided into two levels of difficulty. First, if we consider this couplet to be a folk tradition, we cannot determine its reading (*paath*). Prewritten texts in folklore were not always stable. Distinct places had distinct recitations of the same text. Secondly, as per the reading, for sin to be considered pride, *abhiman*, or ego, it would mean that the root of a human's ego is their sin. This is not traditionally accepted. In the Indian knowledge tradition, the body is generally considered the cause of pride or ego. Therefore, Gandhi's reading itself is authentic and represents continuity (personal discussion and communication).

4   RNE: silver ore in a tin mine

5   RNE: one another and

6   RNE: and if this

7   RNE: Australia of whom

8   RNE: take

9   RNE: History does not and cannot take note of this fact.

10 RNE: one of them repents and re-awakens the love that was lying dormant in him, the two again begin to have in peace, nobody takes note of this. But if the two brothers,

11 RNE: families and another

12 History, then, is a record of an interruption of the course of nature. Soul-force, being natural, is not noted in history: 1909-GE: હિસ્ટરી એ અસ્વાભાવિક બીનાની નોંધ લેય છે. સત્યાગ્રહ એ સ્વાભાવિક છે એટલે તેની નોંધ લેવાપણું રહેતું નથી; 1959-HE: हिस्टरी अस्वाभाविक बातों कों दर्ज करतीहै.सत्याग्रह स्वाभाविक है, इसलिए उसे दर्ज करने की जरूरत ही नहीं हैं.હિસ્ટરી એ અસ્વાભાવિક બીનાની નોંધ લેય છે/ हिस्टरी अस्वाभाविक बातों कों दर्ज करती है- It means: history registers unusual developments.

13 RNE: suffering, it

14 RNE: If by using violence I

15 Body-force: 1909- શરીરબળ(sharirbal);1959-HE: शरीर-बल.

16 RNE: law and

17 RNE: No man can claim that he is absolutely in the right or that a particular thing is wrong because he thinks so, but it is wrong for him so long as that is his deliberate judgment. It is therefore meet

18 RNE: what is right and
19 RNE: law-givers, but
20 RNE: religion and
21 1909-GE: સત્યાગ્રહી (satyagrahi); 1959-HE: સત્યાગ્રહી.
22 RNE: compliant that
23 Manhood: 1909-GE: માણસાઈ (maanasai); જે માણસ પોતે માણસાઈમાં છે, જેને ખુદાનોજ ડર છે તે બીજાથી ડરવાનો નથી (the man who has realised his humanity, who fears only God, will fear no-one else); 1959-ઇન્સાનિયત; humanity, civility.
24 RNE: fear no one
25 RNE: So low that we fancy
26 RNE: It is a superstition and ungodly
27 RNE: wrong and
28 RNE: robbers a knowledge
29 Brute-force: 1909-GE: શરીરબળ (sharirbal); 1959-HE: શરીર-બલ.
30 Gun-powder: 1909-GE: દારૂગોળો (darugolo); 1959-HE:ગોલા-બારૂદ.
31 RNE: gunpowder, is
32 RNE: From what you say I deduce that passive resistance is a splendid weapon of the weak, but that when they are strong they may take up arms.
33 RNE: English and
34 RNE: bosom-friend, or he
35 Manhood: 1909-GE: માણસાઈ (maanasai); 1959-ઇન્સાનિયત; humanity, civility.
36 Jiu-jitsu: 1909-GE:મલકુસ્તી(malkusti); 1959-HE: કુશ્તી; Jiu-jitsu is a modern Japanese art.
37 RNE: necessary, and when
38 RNE: sword, it can be used anyhow, it
39 RNE: blood it
40 RNE: rusts and

41 RNE: To me it means its teeming millions on whom depends the existence of its princes and our own.

42 RNE: want guns, and

43 RNE: madmen

44 Principality: 1909-GE: રાજસ્થાન (Rajasthan).

45 Villagers: 1909-GE: રઈત (રૈયત-*raiyat*); 1959-HE: रैयत. Gandhi uses ryots and villagers interchangeably. Ryots are peasants or tenant farmers.

46 Real home rule is possible only where passive resistance is the guiding force of the people. Any other rule is foreign rule: In the Gujarati edition, real swaraj exists wherein raiyats/villagers offer satyagraha aagainst unjust laws or dictums. Swaraj is used for "real home rule" and foreign rule is *kuraj*.

47 RNE: mind there

48 RNE: If I were to ask a man with a shattered body to face a cannon's mouth I should make a laughing-stock of myself.

49 RNE: I should like you to explain how a man may become one.

50 RNE: To become a passive resister is easy enough but it is also equally difficult. I have known a lad of fourteen years become a passive resister, I have known also sick people do likewise; and I have also known physically strong and otherwise happy people unable to take up passive resistance. After a great deal of experience it seems to me that those who want to become passive resisters for the service of the country have to observe perfect chastity, adopt poverty, follow truth, and cultivate fearlessness.

51 RNE: to do is

52 RNE: naturally,

53 RNE: indulgence because

54 RNE: Several questions arise: How is one to carry one's wife with one, what are her rights, and other similar questions.

55 RNE: followed and

56 RNE: bodily injuries or death.
57 RNE: chastity and
58 RNE: lion and
59 RNE: stick and

Chapter 18: Education

1 1909-GE: કેળવણી (*kelavani*); 1959-HE: शिक्षा.
2 RNE: education, we
3 Sayajirao Gaekwad (1863–1939) governed the princely state of Baroda. He believed in economic nationalism, established the technical college Kala Bhavan in 1890 and opened admission to artisans and Dalits, founded the Music School in 1886, offered scholarships to Ambedkar, introduced free and compulsory education in 1906 in the state of Baroda, and rejected the notion of pollution and purity. He is known for his welfare measures towards marginal communities(Mehta, 1993, pp. 403–08).
4 RNE: effort then of
5 RNE: It simply means a knowledge of letters. It is merely an instrument, and an instrument may be well used or abused.
6 RNE: it; and
7 Boys:1909-GE: લોકોને (*lokone*); 1959-HE: लोग; people (it translated as"to teach people")
8 RNE: Fellow villagers
9 1909-GE: પશ્ચિમના પ્રતાપ (*Paschimna pratap*); 1959-HE: पश्चिम का असर; influence of the West.
10 RNE: Carried away by the flood of Western thought we
11 Thomas Henry Huxley (1825–95) was a well-known scientist and science promoter who wrote his famous essay in 1868 on *A Liberal Education and Where To Find It*. The full quote is as follows:

That man, I think, has had a liberal education, who has been so trained in youth that his body is the ready servant of his will, and does with ease and pleasure all the work that, as a mechanism, it is capable of; whose intellect is a clear, cold, logic engine, with all its parts of equal strength, and in smooth working order; ready, like a steam engine, to be turned to any kind of work, and spin the gossamers as well as forge the anchors of the mind; whose mind is stored with a knowledge of the great and fundamental truths of Nature and of the laws of her operations; one who, no stunted ascetic, is full of life and fire, but whose passions are trained to come to heel by a vigorous will, the servant of a tender conscience; who has learned to love all beauty, whether of Nature or of art, to hate all vileness, and to respect others as himself.

Such an one and no other, I conceive, has had a liberal education; for he is, as completely as a man can be, in harmony with Nature. He will make the best of her, and she of him (Huxley, 1911, p. 36)

12 RNE: I claim to have become free from its ill effect, and I am trying to give you the benefit of my experience and, in doing so, 1 am demonstrating the rottenness of this education.

13 RNE: use and it

14 RNE: In its place it can be of use and it has its place when we have brought our senses under subjection and put our ethics on a firm foundation.

15 RNE: in it and

16 RNE: Macaulay;

17 RNE: trying each division to

18 RNE: George, is

19 RNE: men

20 RNE: a medium, that when I become a barrister, I may not speak my mother-tongue

21 RNE: English-knowing Men: 1909-GE: અંગ્રેજી જાણનાર (*Angreji jananar*/ proficient in English); 1959-HE: अंग्रेजी जाननेवाले; RNE: English-knowing Indians.

22 Curse of the nation: 1909-GE: પ્રજાની હાય ; 1959-HE: राष्ट्र की हाय; *Praja* is used in a wider sense, i.e. nation.

23 RNE: how disgusted

24 RNE: Every cultured Indian will know in addition to his own provincial language, if a Hindu, Sanskrit, if a Mahomedan, Arabic; if a Parsee, Persian, and all, Hindi.

25 Northerners and Westerners: Northern and Western India.

26 RNE: us, slaves

27 RNE: this land

28 RNE: selfish, they

29 A Zoroastrian/Parsee priest.

30 RNE: hands, but if they will

31 RNE: polluted and it

32 RNE: ourselves because

33 RNE: In our own civilization there will naturally be progress, retrogression, reforms, and reactions,

Chapter 19: Machinery

1 1909-GE: સંચા કામ (*sancha kaam*); 1959-HE: मशीनें. સંચા કામ refers to machines (Montgomery, Desai & Desai, 1877, p. 514).

In Gujarati, both Sancha (સંચા) and Yantra (યંત્ર) are commonly employed to refer to machines or any other object that minimises manual labour. For instance, in Gujarati, the terms for a sharpener, sewing machine and spinning wheel are together referred to as "sancho" (સંચો). However, it seems that Gandhi employed the phrase "Sancha Kaam" (સંચા કામ) to refer to any mechanical activity.

I am grateful to Mahendra Parmar for the aforesaid suggestion.

2 RNE: question, you

3 RNE: When I read Mr. Dutt's Economic History of India, I wept, and as I think of it again my heart sickens.

4   One of the earliest

5   RNE: blamed?

6   RNE: clothmills

7   RNE: true Bengal

8   RNE: cloth than

9   our money; but

10   Gandhi uses the words "Indian Rockefeller" and "American Rockefeller" as general expressions to effectively illustrate the characteristics of capitalists and capital. John D. Rockefeller (1839–1937) was an American businessman noted for his charitable endeavours.

11   RNE: any India

12   RNE: we shall have

13   RNE: rule, their

14   RNE: The other thing which is equally harmful is sexual vice.

15   RNE: body but

16   RNE: handlooms and

17   RNE: Whether the millowners do this or not people

18   RNE: cloth but

19   Statue of god.

20   RNE: So doing, we shall save our eyes and money and support Swadeshi and so shall we attain Home Rule.

21   RNE: It is not to be conceived that all men will do all these things at one time or that some men will give up all machine-made things at once. But, if the thought is sound, we shall always find out what we can give up and gradually cease to use it. What a few may do, others will copy; and the movement will grow like the coconut of the mathematical problem. What the leaders do, the populace will gladly do in turn. The matter is neither complicated nor difficult. You and I need not wait until we can carry others with us. Those will be the losers who will not do it, and those who will not do it, although they appreciate the cowards.

22 RNE: cities and

23 RNE: railways, and

24 RNE: boast of

25 RNE: the doctors went down and people were less unhealthy.

26 RNE: This is one of those instances which demonstrate that sometimes poison is used to kill poison. This, then, will not be a good point regarding machinery. As it expires, the machinery, as it were, says to us: "Beware and avoid me You will derive no benefits from me and the benefit that may accrue from printing will avail only those who are infected with the machinery craze."

27 RNE: Do not, therefore, forget the main thing. It is necessary to realize that machinery is bad. We shall then be able gradually to do away with it. Nature has not provided any way whereby we may reach a desired goal all of a sudden. If, instead of welcoming machinery as a boon, we should look upon it as an evil, it would ultimately go.

Chapter 20: Conclusion

1 1909-GE: છુટકારો (*Chhutkaro*); 1959:HE-छुटकारा; છુટકારો denotes to "emancipation" (Montgomery, Desai & Desai, 1877, p. 514).

2 RNE: And how can those who want only to serve have a party?

3 Where I differ from them, I would respectfully place my position before them and continue my service.

4 Foreign Rule: 1909-GE: પરરાજ્ય (*par-rajya*); 1959-HE: परराज्य.

5 RNE: Home Rule if you have merely expelled the English

6 RNE: to Indian soil.

7 RNE: India, bag and baggage

8 RNE: so-called

9 RNE: Rule

10 RNE: Home Rule

11 RNE: my country but although

12 RNE: you support to be the reverse of civilization

13 RNE: your advantage and, if

14 RNE: It is your duty as rulers that for the sake of the Hindus you should eschew beef, and for the sake of the Mahomedans you should avoid bacon and ham.

15 RNE: nothing because

16 RNE: When she comes we shall look after her. If you are with us, we may then receive her jointly. We do not need any European cloth. We shall manage with articles produced and manufactured at home.

> Concerning *"We do not need any European cloth"*, Gujarati and Hindi editions read it as "We do not want foreign and any European cloth".

17 RNE: unable to do so, but if

18 RNE: If you act contrary to our will, we shall not help you; and without our help, we know that you cannot move one step forward.

19 RNE: you at once; but if

20 RNE: We believe that at heart you belong to a religious nation.

21 RNE: You, English, who have come to India are not good specimens of the English nation, nor can we, almost half Anglicised Indians, be considered good specimens of the real Indian nation.

22 RNE: in India; and if

23 RNE: you and you

24 RNE: doing, we

25 I have been thinking of, that is those

26 RNE: civilization and

27 RNE: the European

28 European is a nine day's wonder: 1909-GE: યુરોપી સુધારો તે ત્રણ દહાડાનો તમાસો છે. (European civilisation is the

spectacle of the three days); 1959-HE:यूरोप का सुधार तीन रोज का तमाशा हैं/ Europe's civilisation is a three-day spectacle.

29 RNE: so imbued who, having experienced

30 RNE: English and

31 RNE: effort and

32 RNE: These are not demands, but they show our mental state. We shall get nothing by asking; we shall have to take what we want, and we need the requisite strength for the effort and that strength will be available to him only who will act thus:

33 RNE: He will only on rare occasions make use of the English language;

34 RNE: If a lawyer, he will give up his profession, and take up a hand-loom;

35 RNE: If a lawyer, he will devote his knowledge to enlightening both his people and the English;

36 RNE: If a lawyer, he will not meddle with the quarrels between parties but will give up the courts, and from his experience induce the people to do likewise;

37 RNE: If a lawyer, he will refuse to be a judge, as he will give up his profession;

38 RNE: If a doctor, he will give up medicine, and understand that rather than mending bodies, he should mend souls;

39 RNE: If a doctor, he will understand that no matter to what religion he belongs, it is better that bodies remain diseased rather than that they are cured through the instrumentality of the diabolical vivisection that is practised in European schools of medicine;

40 RNE: Although a doctor, he will take up a hand-loom, and if any patients come to him, will tell them the cause of their diseases, and will advise them to remove the cause rather than pamper them by giving useless drugs; he will understand that if by not taking drugs, perchance the patient dies, the

world will not come to grief and that he will have been really merciful to him;

41 RNE: Although a wealthy man, yet regardless of his wealth, he will speak out his mind and fear no one;

42 RNE: If a wealthy man, he will devote his money to establishing hand-looms, and encourage others to use hand-made goods by wearing them himself:

43 RNE: Like every other Indian, he will know that this is a time for repentance, expiation and mourning;

44 RNE: Like every other Indian, he will know that to blame the English is useless that they came because of us, and remain also for the same reason, and that they will cither go or change their nature only when we reform ourselves;

45 RNE: Like others, he will understand that at a time of mourning, there can be no indulgence, and that, whilst we are in a fallen state, to be in gaol or in banishment is much the best;

46 RNE: Like others, he will know that it is superstition to imagine it necessary that we should guard against being imprisoned in order that we may deal with the people;

47 RNE: Like others, he will know that action is much better than speech, that it is our duty to say exactly what we think and face the consequences and that it will be only then that we shall be able to impress anybody with our speech;

48 RNE: Like others, he will understand that we shall become free only through suffering;

49 The British Government established a penal settlement in the Andaman and Nicobar Islands. This was known as Cellular Jail, or infamously *Kala Pani*. "The Andaman penal system is sui generis *i.e.* it has grown up on its own lines. It has always been independent of the Indian prison system and has been gradually adopted to the requirements of the situation...It was only ten years after the establishment of the settlement that attention was paid to draft a set of rules and ultimately rules

of the Governor General in Council for the management of transported convicts under Section 34 of Act V of 1871 (prisoners) were framed on 29 July 1874." (Mathur, 1968, p. 150). "By the beginning of 1897 about 400 cells were ready for occupation in the newly constructed Cellular Jail at Aberdeen. It was, therefore, decided to put into effect the system of separate confinement for the first six months. The Cellular Jail was completed by end of 1910 consisting of 663 cells . . . In 1905, the Superintendent, Port Blair was authorised by the Government of India to curtail, suspend or remit such portion of incarceration in Cellular Jail of a convict as he deemed fit and to transfer the convict to the next stage . . . "(Mathur, 1968, p. 157).

There were 149 political prisoners in the Cellular Jail from 1909 to 1921 (http://db.and.nic.in/cellularjail/Stories/NewIndex22.htm). In June 1909, In June 1909, Ganesh Damodar Savarkar (1879–1945) was sentenced to be transported to the cellular jail. A close associate of the V.D. Savarkar (1883–1966), Madanlal Dhingra (1883–1909) killed Sir Curzon Willey in London on 1 July 1909. Ganesh Savarkar was imprisoned in the cellular jail from 1910 to 1922. His younger brother, Vinayak Damodar Savarkar, was in a cellular jail from 1911 to 1921.

50 RNE: Like others, he will understand that deportation for life to the Andamans is not enough expiation for the sin of encouraging European civilization;

51 RNE: Like others, he will know that no nation has risen without suffering, that. even in physical warfare, the true test is suffering and not the killing of others, much more so in the warfare of passive resistance;

52 RNE: Like others, he will know that it is an idle excuse to say that we shall do a thing when the others also do it; that we should do what we know to be tight, and that others will do it

when they see the way, that when I fancy a particular delicacy, I do not wait till others taste it: that to make a national effort and to suffer are in the nature of delicacies, and that to suffer under pressure is no suffering.

53 RNE: retaliate, but

Appendices: Some Authorities

1 RNE: Civilization
2 RNE: Civilization

Testimonies by Eminent Men

1 RNE: The following extracts from Mr. Alfred Webb's valuable collection show that the ancient Indian civilization has little to learn from the modern:
2 Second in RNE
3 First in RNE
4 Third in RNE
5 Deleted in RNE
6 Seventh in RNE
7 Fourth in RNE
8 Eighth in RNE
9 Sixth in RNE
10 Fifth in RNE

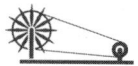

REFERENCES

Ammer, Christine. 2013. *The American Heritage Dictionary of Idioms*. Boston: Houghton Mifflin Harcourt.

Austin, John. 1861. *The Province of Jurisprudence Determined: The First Part of A Series Of Lectures on Jurisprudence, Or the Philosophy of Positive Law*. London: John Edward Taylor, Little Queen Street, Lincoln's Inn Fields.

Chakrabarty, Dipesh and Rochona Majumdar. 2013. "Gandhi's Gita and Politics as Such". In *Political Thought in Action: The Bhagavad Gita and Modern India*, ed. Shruti Kapila and Faisal Devji. Cambridge: Cambridge University Press.

Chaturvedi, Vinayak. 2022. *Hindutva and Violence: V.D. Savarkar and the Politics of History*. Albany: SUNY Press.

CWMG IX. 1963. "My Third Experience in Goal-II", pp. 238–43. New Delhi: The Publications Division, Ministry of Information and Broadcasting, Government of India.

CWMG LXV. 1976. "Speech at Gandhi Seva Sangh Meeting", Hudli-II. New Delhi: The Publications Division, Ministry of Information and Broadcasting, Government of India, pp. 99–106).

CWMG LXXI. 1978. "Speech at Gandhi Seva Sangh Meeting"-I, pp. 232–50. New Delhi: The Publications Division, Ministry of Information and Broadcasting, Government of India.

CWMG LXXXVIII. 1983. "Speech at Prayer Meeting". New Delhi: The Publications Division, Ministry of Information and Broadcasting, Government of India.

CWMG V. 1961. "Joseph Mazzini: A Remarkable Career", pp. 27–28. New Delhi: The Publications Division, Ministry of Information and Broadcasting, Government of India.

CWMG VII. 1962. "Servants of India", p. 14. New Delhi: The Publications Division, Ministry of Information and Broadcasting, Government of India.

CWMG XLVIII. 1971. "Extracts from Proceedings of the Federal Structure Committee Meeting", pp. 215–20. New Delhi: The Publications Division, Ministry of Information and Broadcasting, Government of India.

CWMG XVII. 1965. "A Humble Suggestion", pp. 395–96. New Delhi: The Publications Division, Ministry of Information and Broadcasting, Government of India.

CWMG XXVIII. 1968. "The Meaning of Gita", pp. 315–21. New Delhi: The Publications Division, Ministry of Information and Broadcasting, Government of India.

CWMG XXXII, 1969. "Discourses on the Gita", pp. 94–376. New Delhi: The Publications Division, Ministry of Information and Broadcasting, Government of India.

Desai, Mahadev, ed. 1946. *The Gospel of Selfless Action,* or *the Gita according to Gandhi* (a translation of the original in Gujarati with an additional introduction and commentary). Ahmedabad: Navajivan.

Desai, Valji Govindji, trans. 1960. *M.K. Gandhi: Discourses on the Gita.* Ahmedabad: Navajivan.

Devji, Faisal. 2012. *The Impossible Indian: Gandhi and the Temptation of Violence*. Cambridge, Mass.: Harvard University Press.

Documentation (1993). *Gandhi Marg 15* (2): 240.

Doke, Joseph J. 1967. *M. K. Gandhi: An Indian Patriot in South Africa*. New Delhi: Publications Division, Ministry of Information and Broadcasting Government of India.

Emerson, Ralph Waldo. 1841. *Self-reliance*. New York: The Roycrofters.

Engels, Frederick. 1887. *The Condition of the Working Class in England in 1844*. New York: John W. Lovell Company.

Gandhi, M.K. 1928. *Satyagraha in South Africa*, trans. Valji Govindji Desai. Madras: S. Ganesan.

Gandhi, M.K. 1960. "Discourses on the Gita", trans. V. G. Desai. Ahmedabad: Navajivan.

Gandhi, M.K. 2018. *An Autobiography or the Story of My Experiments with Truth*, introduced with notes by Tridip Suhrud. Gurgaon: PRHI.

Gandhi, M.K. 22 September 1920. "Swaraj in One Year", *Young India* II (38):1–2.

Gandhi, M.K. 26 January 1921. "Hind Swaraj or the Indian Home Rule", *Young India* 3 (4): 27–28.

Gandhi, M.K. 6 August 1931. "The message of the Gita", pp. 205–07. *Young India* 13 (32).

Gandhi, Rajmohan. 2006. *Mohandas: A True Story of a Man, His People and an Empire*. New Delhi: Penguin.

Gowda K., Nagappa. 2011. *The Bhagavadgita in the Nationalist Discourse*. New Delhi: Oxford University Press.

Growse, F. S. 1914. *The Ramayana of Tulsi Das*, sixth edition. Allahabad: Ram Narain Lal, Publisher & Bookseller.

Hofmeyr, Isabel. 2013. *Gandhi's Printing Press: Experiments in Slow Reading*. Cambridge, Mass.: Harvard University Press.

Homer. 1919. *The Odyssey*. Trans. A.T. Murray. Cambridge, Mass.: Harvard University Press.

Hunt, James D. 1993. *Gandhi in London, revised edition*. New Delhi: Promila & Co., Publishers.

Huxley, Thomas Henry. 1911. *Selections from Huxley*. Boston: Ginn and Company.

Jordens, J.T.F. 1986. "Gandhi and the Bhagavadgita". In *Modern Indian Interpreters of the Bhagavadgita*, ed. Robert N. Minor, pp. 88–109. Albany: State University of New York Press, 1986.

Keer, Dhananjay. 1973. *Mahatma Gandhi: Political Saint and Unarmed Prophet*. Bombay: Popular Prakashan.

Kher, S.B., ed. 1996. *The Law and the Lawyers : M.K. Gandhi*. Ahmedabad: Navajivan.

Kopf, David. 1979. *The Brahmo Samaj and the Shaping of the Modern Indian Mind*. Princeton: Princeton University Press.

Krishna, Daya. 1991. *Indian Philosophy: A Counter Perspective*. Delhi: Oxford University Press.

Kumar, Aishwarya. 2015. *Radical Equality. Ambedkar, Gandhi, and the Risk of Democracy*. Stanford: Stanford University.

Lutgendorf, Philip, trans. 2016. *Tulsidas: The Epic of Ram*. Cambridge, Mass.: Murti Classic Library and Harvard University Press.

Macaulay, T.B. 1862. "Minute by Mr. Macaulay". In H. Woodrow, *Minutes on Education in India*, pp. 105–16. Calcutta: C. B. Lewis, at the Baptist Mission Press.

Martin, Jr., Briton. 1969. *New India, 1885: British Official Policy and the Emergence of the Indian National Congress*. Berkeley California: University of California Press.

Mathur, Laxman Prasad. 1968. *History of the Andaman and Nicobar Islands (1756-1966)*. Delhi: Sterling Publishers (P) Ltd.

Mehta, Makrand. "Princely Ruler as an Agent of Change: A Study of Maharaja Sayajirao Gaekwad's Policies Towards Untouchability, 1882-1915". In *Proceedings of the Indian History Congress, 54* (1993): 403–08.

Mehta, Uday Singh. 1999. *Liberalism and Empire: A Study in Nineteenth-Century British Liberal Thought*. Chicago: The University of Chicago Press.

Misra, B.B. 1963. *Select Documents on Mahatma Gandhi's Movement in Champaran 1917-18*. Patna: The Government of Bihar.

Montgomery, Robert, Ambalal Sakerlal Desai and Manidharprasad Tapiprasad Desai. 1877. *A Dictionary, English and Gujarati, Compiled for the Bombay Government Educational Department*. Surat: The Irish Presbyterian Mission Press.

Naoroji, Dadabhai. 1901. *Poverty and Un-British Rule in India*. London: Swan Sonnenschein & Co., LIM, Paternoster Square.

Parekh, Bhikhu. 1999. *Colonialism, Tradition and Reform: An Analysis of Gandhi's Political Discourse, revised edition*. New Delhi: Sage Publications.

Parel, Anthony J., ed. 1997. *Hind Swaraj and Other Writings*. Cambridge: Cambridge University Press.

Parel, Anthony J. 2007. *Gandhi's Philosophy and the Quest for Harmony*. Cambridge: Cambridge University Press.

Parel, Anthony J. 2016. *Pax Gandhiana: The Political Philosophy of Mahatma Gandhi*. New York: Oxford University Press.

Rai, Dhananjay. 2023. *Poorna Swaraj: Constructive Programme: Its Meaning and Place by M.K. Gandhi*. Gurgaon: PRHI.

Ramcharitmanas. 2022. Gorakhpur: Gita Press.

Sarkar, Sumit. 2014. *Modern India (1885-1947)*. Delhi: Pearson.

Seal, Anil. 1971. *The Emergence of Indian Nationalism: Competition and Collaboration in the Later Nineteenth Century*. Cambridge: Cambridge University Press.

Shah, K.J. 1992. "Of Artha and the Arthasastra', in *Comparative Political Philosophy: Studies Under the Upas Tree*, ed. Anthony J Parel and Ronald C Keith, pp. 141–62. New Delhi: SAGE.

Shah, K.J. 1996. "Purushartha and Gandhi', in *Gandhi and the Present Global Crisis*, ed. Ramashray Roy, pp. 155–61. Shimla: Indian Institute of Advanced Study.

Sharma, Suresh and Tridip Suhrud, ed. 2010. *M.K. Gandhi's Hind Swaraj: A Critical Edition* New Delhi: Orient BlackSwan.

Skaria, Ajay. 2016. *Unconditional Equality: Gandhi's Religion of Resistance*. Minneapolis: University of Minnesota Press.

Stallard, Matthew. 3 June 2023. "Cotton Capital: How Slavery Made Manchester the World's First Industrial City". *Guardian*. https://www.theguardian.com/news/ng-interactive/2023/apr/03/cotton-capital-how-slavery-made-manchester-the-worlds-first-industrial-city.

Tendulkar, D.G. 1960. *Mahatma: Life of Mohandas Karamchand Gandhi, Volume One: 1869–1920*. New Delhi: Publication Division, Government of India.

Veeravalli, Anuradha. 2011. "Swaraj and Sovereignty", *Economic and Political Weekly* 46(5): 65–69.

Zaehner, R.C. 1966. *Hinduism*. Oxford: Oxford University Press.

Zaidi, A. Moin and Shaheda Zaidi, ed. 1976. *The Encyclopaedia of the Indian National Congress, Volume One: 1885-1890 The Founding Fathers*. Delhi: S. Chand and Company Ltd.

Scan QR code to access the
Penguin Random House India website